"Wearing black to mask their identities, the Black Bloc fights injustice globally. Although little is known about these modern Zorros, this book critically reveals their origins and prospects. I heartily recommend it."

> —George Katsiaficas, activist and author of *The Subversion of Politics*

"Dupuis-Déri cuts through the crap, taking the Black Bloc tactic seriously as both a political tool and a manifestation of the rage and joy that are part of the struggle for a better world."

> —Lesley J. Wood, Professor of Sociology, York University, and author of *Direct Action, Deliberation, and Diffusion*

"The richness, imaginativeness, and sheer learning of Francis Dupuis-Déri's work is stimulating and impressive. The whole book turns on a fascinating blend of the rigorously analytical and the generously imaginative. It was high time that it should be translated into English, as this well-established anarchist classic will both delight and inform."

> —Andrej Grubacic, Professor of Anthropology and Social Change, California Institute of Integral Studies, and co-author of *Wobblies & Zapatistas*

"*Who's Afraid of the Black Blocs?* is a measured, critical, and persuasive defence of global protest actions. Against critics who dismiss these as purposeless or who treat illegalism as a distraction to the mainstream event, Dupuis-Déri highlights the effectiveness of the Black Blocs decision-making processes and the considered politics of its participants."

> —Ruth Kinna, Professor of Politics, History and International Relations, Loughborough University, UK and author of *Anarchism: A Beginner's Guide*

"Francis Dupuis-Déri provides the most sustained, energetic, and exciting discussion of the Black Blocs yet. No other work brings together the voices of participants and supporters, critics (from inside and outside of the movements), academics, and public commentators in such thorough analysis. His approach takes Black Blocs seriously but is in no way uncritical. This is essential reading for anyone concerned with contemporary political strategies and tactics. It will be urgently read by anyone seeking a glimpse of politics beyond the bland and rote repetition of conventional and familiar protest politics. Read it before your next demo."

—Jeff Shantz, author of *Commonist Tendencies*

"At last, a thorough historical and political explanation of property destruction as social protest."

—Amory Starr, author of *Naming the Enemy, Global Revolt*, and *Shutting down the Street*

"Francis Dupuis-Déri is one of the most important radical thinkers of his generation. This noteworthy translation of his groundbreaking analysis of the Black Blocs is a most welcome addition to scholarship. It is exemplary of his unwavering commitment to the serious study of emancipatory politics."

—Martin Breaugh, Associate Professor of Political Science, York University and author of *The Plebeian Experience*

WHO'S AFRAID OF THE

BLACK BLOCS?

ANARCHY IN ACTION AROUND THE WORLD

FRANCIS DUPUIS-DÉRI

Translated by Lazer Lederhendler

Who's Afraid of the Black Blocs? Anarchy in Action Around the World
By Francis Dupuis-Déri

Originally published in French as *Les Black Blocs. La liberté et l'égalité se manifestent* © Lux Éditeur, Montréal, 2007 www.luxediteur.com
English translation ©2013 Lazer Lederhendler
This edition © PM Press 2014
All rights reserved. No part of this book may be transmitted by any means without permission in writing from the publisher.

ISBN: 978-1-60486-949-1
Library of Congress Control Number: 2014908058

Cover design by John Yates
Front cover photo by Neal Rockwell
Layout by David Vereschagin/Quadrat Communications

PM Press
PO Box 23912
Oakland, CA 94623
www.pmpress.org

First published in English translation in 2013 by
Between the Lines
401 Richmond Street West, Studio 277
Toronto, Ontario M5V 3A8
Canada
www.btlbooks.com

10 9 8 7 6 5 4 3 2 1

Printed by the Employee Owners of Thomson-Shore in Dexter, Michigan.
www.thomsonshore.com

CONTENTS

PREFACE

The French edition of this book first appeared in 2003 and was followed by two more in 2005 and 2007. This first English edition has been updated to take into account the events of the past decade. Over the years I have had the privilege of speaking with activists with a variety of opinions and personal histories. The conversations took place on four occasions: the Quebec student strike of 2012, the mobilization against the 2010 G20 Summit in Toronto (I was a member of CLAC, the Convergence des luttes anticapitalistes, based in Montreal), the one against the G8 meeting in Évian in 2003, and the protests against the Summit of the Americas in Quebec City in 2001. During those events I was also able to meet with close observers of the movement, including Clément Barrette, who in 2002 authored a study titled *La pratique de la violence politique par l'émeute: le cas de la violence exercée lors des contre-sommets* (The practice of political violence through rioting: the case of the counter-summits). Following the publication of the second edition of *Les blacks blocs* by the Atelier de création libertaire in Lyon in the spring of 2005, a number of collectives in a dozen cities in France and Switzerland generously invited me to discuss the Black Blocs phenomenon. At the information booths set up at these meetings I was able to stock up on pamphlets dealing with marches and direct action. This literature and the lively debates in which I took part prompted me to include in this edition additional statements by demonstrators who had participated in Black Blocs. I was also able to integrate (thanks to translation assistance from Davide Pulizzotto) information drawn from *Black Blocs*, a book published in Italian in 2011. I would like to thank the photographers for their permission to use their work. I would also like to thank Amanda Crocker, Marie-Éve Lamy, Lazer Lederhendler, and Matthew Kudelka for their alert readings and comments. Finally, apologies are in order for any overlap between this book and three previously published articles of mine: "The Black Blocs Ten Years After Seattle," *Journal for the Study of Radicalism* 4, no. 2 (2010); "Penser l'action directe des Black Blocs," *Politix* 17, no. 68 (December 2004); and "Black Blocs: bas les masques," *Mouvements* 25 (January–February 2003).

⚑ INTRODUCTION

... never seen except when feared ...
Don't forget: they hit the streets ...
  —Léo Ferré, *Les anarchistes*

The Black Blocs are today's best political philosophers.
  —Nicolas Tavaglione

One day, history will vindicate us.
  —Black Bloc participant, Toronto, June 2010

Amid clouds of tear gas, police officers in full riot gear face off with silhouetted figures bustling in the street. Masked and dressed in black, those figures are the "Black Bloc." The black flag of anarchism waves above the commotion as bottles, rocks, and even the occasional Molotov cocktail fly overhead. The police fire volleys of tear gas and rubber bullets. Sometimes the bullets are real. The action unfolds against a backdrop of banks and multinational retail shops smeared with anarchist and anti-capitalist graffiti, their windows shattered. Since the epic "Battle of Seattle," fought on November 30, 1999, during the meeting of the World Trade Organization (WTO), the media have enthusiastically captured such scenes.

According to a widespread myth, there is only one Black Bloc, which is thought to be a single permanent organization with numerous branches throughout the world. In fact, the term Black Bloc represents

The Black Bloc tactic allows individuals to retain their anonymity by wearing masks and head-to-toe black clothing. May 1, 2013, Berlin.

a shifting, ephemeral reality. Black Blocs are composed of ad hoc assemblages of individuals or affinity groups that last for the duration of a march or rally. The expression designates a specific type of collective action, a tactic that consists in forming a mobile bloc in which all individuals retain their anonymity thanks in part to their masks and head-to-toe black clothing. Black Blocs may occasionally use force to express their outlook in a demonstration, but more often than not they are content to march peacefully. The primary objective of a Black Bloc is to embody within the demonstration a radical critique of the economic and political system. Metaphorically speaking, it is a huge black flag made up of living bodies, flying in the heart of a demonstration. As one activist put it, "the Black Bloc is our banner."[1] To make their message more explicit, Black Blocs generally display a number of anarchist flags (black or red and black) and banners bearing anti-capitalist and anti-authoritarian slogans.

There is no social body organized on a permanent basis that answers or lays claim to the name Black Bloc, although on occasion people involved in a Black Bloc have released an anonymous communiqué after a protest to explain and justify their deeds. More recently, in 2013, Facebook pages associated with the Black Blocs in Egypt and in Brazil offered explanations about civil disobedience, justifications for resorting to force in street protests, and criticisms of the structural violence of capitalism and the state system.

Voices decrying the "theoretical confusion" and "theoretical poverty" of Black Blocs and their allies can be heard even on the far left.[2] But this sort of criticism is specious, because it assesses the theoretical value of direct actions using criteria that are foreign to such gestures, comparing them, for instance, to treatises of social or political philosophy. For many of its participants, the Black Bloc tactic enables them to express a world view and a radical rebuke of the political and economic system, yet they are certainly not so credulous as to believe that doing so can frame a general theory of liberal society and globalization. The Black Bloc is not a treatise in political philosophy, let alone a strategy; it is a tactic. A tactic is not about global power relations, or about how to take power, or even better, how to get rid of power and domination. A tactic is not about global revolution. Does this imply renouncing political thinking and action? No. A tactic such as the Black Bloc is a way of behaving in street protests. It may help empower the people protesting in the street, by giving them the opportunity to express a radical critique of the system, or by strengthening their ability to resist the police's assaults on the people.

By and large, the men and women who take part in Black Blocs assign a clear political meaning to their direct actions. Their tactic, when it involves the use of force, enables them to show the "public" that neither private property nor the state, as represented by the police, is sacred, and to indicate that some are prepared to put themselves in harm's way to express their anger against capitalism or the state, or their solidarity with those most disadvantaged by the system. A woman who had participated in many Black Blocs told me their actions against businesses and media vehicles are designed "to show we don't want companies and media with unbelievable profit rates and that benefit from free trade at the expense of the population."[3] The Black Bloc type of action falls largely within the bounds of the media spectacle, inasmuch as it strives to introduce a counter-spectacle, albeit one somehow dependent on the official spectacle and public and private media.[4] A participant in a Black Bloc in Toronto in 2010 put it this way: "The Black Bloc will not make the revolution. It would be naive to think that, in itself, the selective targeting of private property can change things. It remains propaganda of the deed."[5]

A Black Bloc can vary in size from a few individuals to hundreds. During the Quebec student strike of 2012, it was not uncommon for people to refer to a lone individual wearing the appropriate outfit as "a Black Bloc." In some cases, several Black Blocs are at work simultaneously during a single event. This happened, for example, at the marches protesting the Quebec City Summit of the Americas in April 2001. The largest Black Blocs are still found in Germany, where the participants number from a few hundred to several thousand. In principle, anyone dressed in black can join the black contingent. At the "anti-cuts" marches held in London on March 31, 2011, one member of the Black Bloc explained: "We had no idea of the numbers before the event on Saturday, and no idea it would be so radical in its actions. The black bloc idea spread like a ripple through the march. As people saw others in black, they changed into black themselves. Some marchers even left the protest to buy black clothing."[6] That said, calls to form a Black Bloc are sometimes sent out into cyberspace as part of a major mobilization, as was the case ahead of the 2001 Summit of the Americas, or by means of wall posters, as in Berlin before May Day of 2013. For very important events, affinity groups may meet hours or days before a demonstration to plan and co-ordinate their actions,

*A Black Bloc at the anti-cut protest in Trafalgar Square, London,
UK, March 26, 2011.*

and co-ordination meetings held weeks or even months in advance
are not unheard of. It is far more common, however, for Black Blocs to
emerge spontaneously.

"Wearing black allows you to strike and then fall back into the
Black Bloc, where you're always just one among many,"[7] a veteran of
various Black Blocs explains, noting that anonymity makes it possible
to partly thwart surveillance by the police, who film all demonstrations
and who requisition images from the media to identify, arrest, and sub-
poena "vandals."[8] Depending on the situation, the same activist adds,
people involved in direct actions may also choose to "disperse, change
clothes, and vanish amid the crowd." This tactic, which proved effective in the follow-ups to the Battle of Seattle, has today lost some of its
surprise effect, making it easier for the police to repress or manipulate
demonstrators who employ it. Nevertheless, it can still be effective at
times, because, for one thing, the police and security services are not
all-powerful and all-controlling.

By 2002, after a number of spectacular events in Washington, Prague, Göteborg, Quebec City, and Genoa, activists like Severino, a member of the Bostonian Barricada Collective of the Northeastern Federation of Anarcho-Communists (NEFAC), were wondering whether "the Black Bloc tactic [had] reached the end of its usefulness."[9] In response to the intense repression following the 9/11 attacks on the United States in 2001, to the relocation of the major international summits to inaccessible venues, and to the outlawing of rallies, others bluntly declared, "the Black Bloc is dead."[10]

Notwithstanding these announcements of its demise, the Black Bloc has revived itself a number of times over the past few years. In September 2003, about a hundred Turkish anarchists organized into Black Blocs marched against "the system and war" on the streets of Ankara. At the end of the event they burned their flags before dispersing.[11] In 2005, a Black Bloc was active in the protest against the G8 in Scotland. In 2007 a Black Bloc of several thousand individuals marched against the G8 in Heilingendamm/Rostock, Germany. Bank windows were broken, a police car vandalized, a Caterpillar office torched—no doubt because Caterpillar equipment was employed to forcibly displace Palestinian communities in Israeli-occupied territories[12]—and 400 police were injured.[13] In the fall of 2008, a Black Bloc went into action in Vichy, France, during the European Union (EU) summit on immigration. Then on December 6, 2008, in Greece, following the death of a 15-year-old anarchist named Alexandros Grigoropoulos at the hands of the Athenian police in the Exarchia district, countrywide demonstrations, in which many Black Bloc contingents took part, often turned into riots. Solidarity marches were held in the Kreutzberg district of Berlin and in Hamburg, where a Black Bloc of several dozen people chanted, "Greece—it was murder! Resistance everywhere!" Similar scenarios played out in Barcelona, where bank windows were shattered; in Madrid, where a police station was attacked; and in Rome, where stones rained down on the Greek embassy.[14] The next year, the Black Bloc tactic was deployed in Strasbourg, during the NATO Summit; in Poitiers, where a prison and some storefronts belonging to Bouygues Telecom were hit; in London, at the G20 (April); and in Pittsburgh, again at the G20 (September). A few months later, in February 2010, a Black Bloc was formed in Vancouver during a rally as part of the "No Olympic Games on Stolen Native Land" campaign. Windows of The Bay department store, a sponsor of the Games, were shattered. The same year, a Black Bloc fought the police during the May Day march in Zurich. Yet in 2010, during the meetings held to prepare for mobilizations against the G20 Summit in Toronto, anti-capitalist militants in Montreal suggested that the Black Bloc belonged to history and that it was time to move on.

Nevertheless, in Toronto, despite nearly a billion dollars spent on security, months of police infiltration efforts, and numerous preventive detentions, a Black Bloc of between 200 and 300 individuals, accompanied by about 1,000 demonstrators, managed to outmanoeuvre the police and smash dozens of display windows along the city's commercial arteries.[15] Within barely an hour, the Black Bloc struck banks and financial services outlets (CIBC, Scotiabank, Western Union),

Heart Attack protest against the 2010 Olympics, West Hastings Street, Vancouver, Canada, February 13, 2010.

multinational telecommunications conglomerates (Rogers, Bell), fast food chains (McDonald's, Starbucks, Tim Hortons), clothing companies (Foot Locker, Urban Outfitters, American Apparel), and an entertainment corporation (HMV),[16] not to mention media vehicles (including those of the CBC) and police property (the Police Museum and four police cars were set on fire, though not all of them by the Black Bloc[17]). Many Torontonians criticized these actions because some small businesses, such as the Horseshoe Tavern and Urbane Cyclist, also sustained damage, apparently for no political reason. By way of a feminist critique, the Zanzibar strip bar was also targeted.[18] A sign over the front entrance had read, "175 sexy dancers—Forget G8 Try G-strings—G20 leaders solve world peace in our VIP rooms."[19] Speaking to a journalist, a protester explained: "This is all part of the sexist, male-dominated war machine we live in."[20] For activists, the political significance of these actions was unmistakable. "This isn't violence," said one. "This is vandalism against violent corporations. We did not hurt anybody. They are the ones hurting people."[21]

In the wake of the Toronto G20 Summit, Black Blocs arose during the anti-austerity mobilizations in London (March 2011); a small Black Bloc was mobilized against the G8 in Deauville, France (May 2011); and a much larger one was formed as part of the "No TAV" movement opposing the construction of a high-speed rail line in the Val di Susa, Italy (July 2011). In September 2011, a Black Bloc took part in the annual human rights march in Tel Aviv. The Occupy Movement, which had put up tents in a number of Western cities in the fall of 2011, called for demonstrations in October of that year. Black Blocs appeared during Occupy rallies in Oakland, where actions were carried out against the Chase Bank, Bank of America, Wells Fargo, Whole Foods Market, and the office of the president of the University of California. Meanwhile, in Rome, Black Blocs targeted several banks and dozens of police officers were injured. In 2012, Black Blocs were seen during the largest and longest student strike in the history of Quebec. There was also a Black Bloc on March 29, 2012, at a general strike against labour law reforms on Plaza Catalunya in Barcelona, and another at a mass rally in Mexico City protesting the inauguration of the new president. Black Blocs were

Black Bloc activists march during the annual human rights march in Tel Aviv, December 9, 2011.

active as well in Greece during the wave of protests against austerity policies. In January 2013 a group calling itself "Black Bloc" (in English) appeared among the demonstrators in Egypt. According to the BBC,

> members of the group appeared in Tahrir Square on 25 January, banging drums and saying they would "continue the revolution" and "defend protesters" ... The Black Bloc describes itself as a group that is "striving to liberate people, end corruption and bring down tyrants" ... Filmed at night, short video shows men wearing black clothes and black masks. Some hold the Egyptian flag while others carry black flags with an "A" sign—an international symbol of anarchism.[22]

In addition, Black Blocs were present at May Day marches in Montreal and Seattle, and a small-scale Black Bloc had confronted the police at the demonstrations against the Chicago NATO summit in May 2012. Finally, in Brazil during the summer of 2013, Black Blocs were involved in street protests in Rio de Janeiro, Sao Paulo, and Belo Horizonte, during the social unrest against the high cost of living.

The black-clad activists known as Black Blocs are not the only masked protesters to be found taking part in contemporary political riots and confrontational demonstrations. Palestinian youths, their faces wrapped in the traditional *keffiyeh*, and armed with no more than stones, have been confronting Israeli soldiers for many years. In Latin America, young *encapuchados* (hooded ones) have long battled with police—for example, during the student mobilizations in Chile.[23] That said, the Black Bloc has drawn special attention and constituted itself as a distinct political subject, in part thanks to its unique aesthetic, but also because it has been associated somewhat indiscriminately with anarchy and destructive irrationality. For instance, a *Toronto Star* report on the mass rally against the G20 identified "anarchists from the notorious Black Blocs," specifying that there were "about 100 Black Bloc anarchists in head-to-foot black clothing, leading an angry mob of about 300 … destroying store fronts and generally creating the kind of havoc they're known for at G8 and G20 summits worldwide."[24]

The fascination with the Black Bloc is such that it has become a "newsworthy" topic. On the day after the major anti-G20 demonstration in Toronto, the *Toronto Star* ran the headline, "Behind the Black Bloc: G20 Violence." A day later, the same newspaper ran a piece titled "Who is the Black Bloc?" When the Black Bloc first appeared in Egypt, in January 2013, the news was covered by the Canadian, French, German, British, Japanese, Israeli, Spanish, Swiss, Tunisian, and US media. In Brazil, there was such a fuss about the Black Bloc that in August 2013 the progressive magazine *Carta Capital* polled its readers with this question: "The Black Bloc, an anti-establishment form of protest, resorts to destruction against banks and stores. What do you think about that? (1) I am against all vandalism at all times. (2) I am in favour of it in the case of stores, if nobody is hurt." The result? 11,835 people answered, 7,793 (66 percent) in favour of the Black Bloc's actions.[25]

Very often, the English words "Black Bloc" are borrowed by other languages. For instance, in Brazil in 2013, the media ran headlines such as "Conheça a estratégia 'Black Bloc,' que influencia protestos no Brasil" (Discover the "Black Bloc" strategy that influenced the demonstrators in Brazil [*G1 Globo*, July 12, 2013]), and "Para especialistas, ideario 'black bloc' permanecera ativo" (Specialists say the ideology "black bloc" remains active [*Folha de S.Paulo*, August 4, 2013]).[26] In Italy on July 4, 2011, following the mobilization of the No TAV movement, newspapers carried front-page headlines such as these: "TAV, guerriglia dei black bloc" (TAV, Black Bloc guerrilla [Rome edition of *Metro*]); "I black bloc contro il cantiere" (Black Bloc against the construction site [*Corriere della Sera*]); and "I black bloc armati venuti de lontano" (Armed Black Blocs come from afar [*La Repubblica*]).[27] Yet some newspapers prefer to translate the English designation into the local language, as when the phrase "Bloque negro" appeared in an *El Pais* report on the protest rallies held in December 2012 at the presidential palace in Mexico City.[28] In Greece, the media and the state coined the term "Koukoulofori" (the hooded ones).

In the weeks and days preceding international summits and other important events, articles in the media focus on the Black Blocs, depicting them, for instance, as "the anarchists who could be the biggest … security threat."[29] When a Black Bloc goes into action, the media's response often follows a recognizable pattern. The same evening or the next morning, editorialists, columnists, and reporters rail against the Black Bloc troublemakers, branding them "thugs." The following day, however, the tone generally becomes more neutral. Readers are informed that anarchists are behind the tactics involving weapons such as rocks, clubs, slingshots, and Molotov cocktails, as well as the use of shields and helmets for defensive purposes. Such articles sometimes allude to major Black Blocs of the past. Then some academics are quoted, as well as representatives of the police and spokespersons for institutionalized social movements, who dissociate themselves from the "vandals." At best, the journalist quotes some participants in the Black Bloc, who then have a chance to speak for themselves and to explain why they do what they do.

Media references to the Black Bloc are sometimes freely adapted for a variety of situations. During the 2012 student strike in Quebec, allusions to the Black Bloc became so commonplace that the term popped up in a column on environmental issues. Deriding the spread of camouflage designs in outdoor apparel, the columnist claimed this makes "rabbits, raccoons, foxes, partridges, and deer scatter like Black Bloc members catching sight of the paddy wagon."[30] In a more serious vein, the disturbances provoked by the Black Bloc at the 2007 G8 were compared by some German media to the positions of certain participants in the official Summit. The *Frankfurter Allgemeine Zeitung*, for example, reported that "the Black Bloc isn't the only group to use this monstrously big annual event as an opportunity to make an impression on the public. Two participants, the American and Russian presidents, already tried to do this by arriving in an unusual way."[31]

The Black Bloc has even become a cultural icon. It has been represented, for instance, in various films. Predictably, the Black Bloc shows up in the 2007 fictional film *Battle in Seattle*, directed by Stuart Townsend. In one sequence a demonstrator shatters the display window of a large store, behind which two female shoppers are talking. Having gotten over her initial surprise, one of the women challenges him: "What are you doing? This woman is pregnant!" He snaps back, "Oh, yeah, you're going to have a kid? ... And you want your kid to work to death in a sweatshop making baby clothes?" "Of course not," the pregnant woman answers. "So don't fucking shop here!" the man yells, before scurrying away. In the next scene a member of the Black Bloc is taken to task by a man and woman who support nonviolent civil disobedience. The ensuing heated debate on violence and the media ends in a scuffle, with the Black Bloc member finally running off to join his comrades. Another instance is the sixth episode of the 2012 season of *Continuum*, a second-rate sci-fi television series, which opens with a scene of pillaging set in the distant future. The pillagers seem to be part of a Black Bloc. A female member of the anti-riot squad laments, "What a waste ... They call themselves revolutionaries but all I see is vandalism, with no respect for private property." Her partner sighs, "If there is a message, I'm not getting it." Later in the episode, the action, now back in the present, has a Black Bloc intruding on a protest rally at the headquarters of a corporation.

An individual reviewing the video recording of the subsequent riot claims to recognize "a guy who I think may be leading the anarchists amongst the legitimate protesters." The opening episode of the second season of the series *XIII* also includes a demonstration featuring a Black Bloc. In *Cosmopolis*, David Cronenberg's film adaptation of Don DeLillo's novel, an anti-capitalist rally has all the trappings of a Black Bloc. A documentary directed by Carlo A. Bachschmidt and released in 2011 under the unadorned title *Black Block*—even though this subject is barely mentioned in the film—deals with the events at the 2001 G8 in Genoa. The Black Bloc has also become the subject of comic books[32] and novels,[33] such as *Black Bloc*, a French detective novel by Elsa Marpeau, published by Gallimard in 2012. In Brian Heagney's *ABCs of Anarchy* (2010), a book for kids, the letter B "is for Black Bloc: A black bloc is a group of people dressed in black to represent either mass solidarity for a cause, or mass resistance to oppression." In a more upscale mode, "Black Block" was the name of the gift shop (closed in 2012) in the contemporary art museum at the Palais de Tokyo in Paris. On sale there were "I Love Black Block" badges and a fashion line including a pair of jeans priced at €240. As indicated on the shop's website, "Blackblock offers clothes in a shop that invites regularly personalities from the world of art, fashion or music to use the space of Blackblock to create their universe."[34]

Certain artists, rather than co-opting the Black Bloc image for commercial or entertainment purposes, use it to make a cogent social statement. This is what the visual artist Francesco di Santis did in the United States, when he produced a series of portraits of Black Bloc activists.[35] Another example is Packard Jennings, an American West Coast artist, who in 2007 created an "Anarchist Action Figure," a 40-centimetre-high figurine representing a young man dressed entirely in black and wearing a black hood. As part of the obvious reference to the Black Bloc, the "action figure" was boxed like a toy together with a few accessories: a gas mask, a jerry can, a paint bomb, and a Molotov cocktail. In addition to the title of the work, the box carried the slogan, "Arm your dissent!" Having deposited the package on the shelf of a toy store, the artist filmed the moment when a customer took it and went to pay for it at the cash register. The artist's aim was to denounce the co-opting of images of radical protest for commercial purposes.[36]

Who Says What About the Black Blocs?

The public image of the Black Blocs has been skewed by the hatred and contempt harboured by their many critics: politicians, police officials, right-wing intellectuals, journalists, academics, the spokespersons for many institutionalized progressive organizations, and other protesters, who feel that they endanger people who are neither able nor prepared to deal with police violence.[37] These detractors are united in denigrating the Black Blocs—or indeed any demonstrators who resort to physical force—portraying them as individuals bereft of political convictions and whose only purpose in joining a demonstration is to satisfy their craving for destruction. Quite often, they are also depicted as coming from afar—for example, from Eugene, Oregon, to protest against the WTO in Seattle, in 1999; from Germany to protest against the G8 in Genoa, in 2001; from Quebec to protest against the G20 in Toronto, in 2010; or from all around Europe, to protest against the TAV in Italy, in 2011.

This derogatory discourse is no surprise, coming from the police. In July 2011, following the disruptive demonstrations of the No TAV movement, police officials stated that "there were about three hundred Black Blocs who had come from Spain, France, Germany, and Austria" with the goal of generating "maximum violence against the authorities." These activists were nothing but "delinquents and cowards" who were "well known to the police and [had] nothing to do with the Val di Susa issue."[38] In London, a few months earlier, Metropolitan Police commander Bob Broadhurst, commenting on the Black Bloc contingent in the "anti-cuts" march, had declared: "I wouldn't call them protesters. They are engaging in criminal activities for their own ends."[39]

Such statements are nothing new. Here, for example, is what Jean-Claude Sauterel, police spokesman in the Vaud district of France, told *Le Figaro* in June 2003, when the G8 leaders were meeting in Évian: "These people have come for the sole purpose of wreaking havoc."[40] His words seemed to echo the statement made ahead of the Summit of the Americas in April 2001 by Florent Gagné, director of the Sûreté du Québec (SQ, Quebec's provincial police force), who said he was concerned about "the so-called direct action groups. These are violent groups with no real ideology. They are vandals, anarchists."[41] That same year, a report by the Office fédéral suisse de la police titled "The potential for violence residing in the antiglobalization movement" was similarly dismissive:

> It is difficult, moreover, to grasp the potential for violence currently displayed by certain youths. Such violence often comes in the shape of a destructive frenzy, apparently unprovoked, or of extreme aggressiveness toward others. Consequently, public events, whatever they may be, are increasingly marred by acts of vandalism devoid of any political or ideological justification.[42]

Explicitly denied here is the political nature of such direct actions, which are thereby cast out beyond the pale of political rationality.

Like the police, politicians attempt to divest the "vandals" of all political reasoning. During the G20 meeting in Toronto, a comment on the website of Canada's left-of-centre political party, the New Democratic Party (NDP), called on progressives to denounce "the Black Bloc thugs. They are not fighting for social justice, they are criminals looking for an excuse to be criminals … A thug is a thug, regardless of their rhetoric."[43] Such criticism sometimes emanates from the upper echelons of the state. In March 2011, following the "anti-cuts" demonstrations in London, British Home Secretary Theresa May said: "I want to condemn in the strongest terms the mindless behaviour of the thugs responsible for the violence."[44] London's Deputy Mayor Kit Malthouse compared the Black Bloc to "fascist agitators," adding that "they were a nasty bunch of black-shirted thugs and it was pretty obvious they were intent on rampaging around and would be difficult to control."[45] In 2010, in the wake of the Toronto G20 Summit, Dimitri Soudas, then head of communications for the Prime Minister of Canada, appealed to patriotic sentiments, declaring that "the thugs that prompted violence earlier today represent in no way, shape or form the Canadian way of life."[46] Already in the early 2000s, politicians were depicting Black Bloc actions as completely lacking in political significance. "I exclude the vandals," said Guy Verhofstadt, the Prime Minister of Belgium and President of the EU, with reference to the G8 Summit in Genoa in July 2001. "They do not express an opinion. They seek violence and that has nothing to do with the G8."[47] German Chancellor Gerhard Schröder, speaking on the same occasion, declared: "It is futile to dialogue with those who have no political beliefs."[48] Meanwhile, the Prime Minister of Canada, Jean Chrétien, stated bluntly that "if the anarchists want to destroy democracy, we won't let them."[49]

Apparently convinced that the Black Blocs have nothing to do with politics, both police officials and politicians have claimed either that they are composed of hooligans, sports fans who surge out of the stadiums and instigate riots (as happened in Rome on the occasion of an Occupy rally in October 2011[50]), or that, on the contrary, sports riots are triggered by anarchists whose only goal is to destroy everything, whatever the occasion. Thus, in 2011, commenting on the riot that had erupted after a defeat of Vancouver's professional hockey team, the Canucks, police chief Jim Chu declared that the rioters were "criminals, anarchists and thugs who came to town bent on destruction and mayhem," terms that would be echoed by the city's mayor, Gregor Robertson, when he pinned the blame for the riot on "anarchists and thugs."[51] Later, however, Chu was obliged to admit he had erred and that anarchists had in no way been involved in the hockey riot.[52]

Journalists are no exception to the rule whereby the actions of "vandals" must be denied any political dimension. Indeed, they sometimes indulge in sneering, categorical value judgments about the Black Blocs and their allies. After the May Day protest of 2012, the *Berlin Kurier,* under the headline "The Hour of the Idiot-Rioters," ran an article that stated: "These hateful fans of chaos [were ready] for rioting and wreckage. They wanted at all cost to do battle in the street!"[53] In 2010, the *Toronto Sun* published a commentary about the G20 demonstrations. This columnist enlisted an "expert" to help readers distinguish between rioters and "real protesters, with a real cause, and real concerns":

In a perfect world, the protests would go on peacefully, people would make their point, whatever the heck that might be, and all would be fine ... As security expert John Thompson of the Mackenzie Institute[54] told me before the summit, there's 2% of the crowd who are there for the criminal free-for-all, with no cause at all.[55]

In an interview with another newspaper, the same John Thompson described people participating in a Black Bloc as "adrenaline junkies ... What the Black Bloc protesters do is basically an extreme sport at public expense." In the same article, concerning the Black Bloc, Peter St. John, a University of Manitoba professor who "specialize[s] in security issues," opined that "when you start using violence, you're really coming under the rubric of a terrorist organization."[56]

Regarding the Black Bloc in Egypt, an *Al Jazeera* article in Arabic reported, on the basis of information from an "anonymous source," that this group had been trained in a military zone of the Negev Desert and was believed to be operating under the supervision of active or retired Israeli secret service officers assisted by Israeli military experts in security and psychology. According to Ibrahim al Brawi, the director of the Palestinian Studies Centre in Cairo, the Egyptian Black Bloc was linked to a global network of human rights organizations and Western security companies and was dedicated to overthrowing the regime.[57] These assertions sound like the figments of highly paranoid imaginations; nevertheless, they have helped construct the public perception of the Black Bloc as a shadowy menace.

The mainstream media consistently describe most demonstrators who resort to force as "very young."[58] Frequent variations include "young extremists,"[59] "young hotheads,"[60] and "young vandals."[61] This line of vilification has been a staple among media professionals since the early 2000s, as illustrated by an Agence France-Presse article asserting that the aim of the "vandals" at Genoa in 2001 was "to destroy everything," and, moreover, that they constituted—as the left-wing intellectual Chris Hedges would echo a few years later—"a veritable cancer within the movement."[62] Regarding the demonstrations in Genoa, French TV news viewers were informed that "the sole objective [of] the notorious Black Blocs," composed of "ultraviolent anarchists" and other "extremists" (who were "thirsting for violence and destruction"), was to "globalize their hate and violence."[63] Five journalists of the French magazine *L'Express* managed to condense into a few lines all the clichés concerning the Black Blocs: "Their discourse, at any rate, is that of anarchism. They advocate the use of violence against anything representing a form of state organization." Rehearsing the stereotypes one by one, the *Express* team observed that "more and more young, somewhat confused Americans" were getting sucked into the Black Bloc phenomenon and eventually involved in demonstrations, "not so much to protest and oppose as to smash and burn."[64]

Journalists also relay the opinions of "ordinary" citizens and "non-violent" demonstrators who disapprove of the use of force. After the 2001 G8, for example, an anonymous resident of Genoa remarked that the "vandals and radicals" had "no specific target in view but simply wanted to destroy things."[65] In another instance, "a sympathiser of the movement" was quoted: "Those people have no political ideas. They represent no one and can be compared to hooligans."[66] Similarly, a reporter covering the demonstrations against the G8 held in France in June 2003 quoted an activist and passed judgement on the Black Bloc at the same time: "Summing up the situation, a sincere alter-globaliz-ation activist dismayed by the disturbances at the marches observed, 'They are motivated only by destruction and vandalism.' The same individual added angrily, 'They are just some little idiots who came to smash windows for the fun of it.'"[67]

Although some spokespersons for mainstream social democratic institutions, such as socialist parties and trade unions,[68] have cen-sured both police violence and the brutality of capitalism, their attacks against the Black Blocs are not unlike those launched by police offi-cials and centrist or rightist politicians. Yvette Cooper, a British Labour MP, when remarking on the above-mentioned events in London, denounced the "few hundred mindless idiots [for engaging in] thug-gish behaviour of the worst kind."[69] Chris Hedges, a progressive antiwar intellectual and writer well known in the United States, had this to say about the Occupy Movement's call for demonstrations in

November 2011: "The Black Bloc anarchists, who have been active in the streets in Oakland and other cities, are the cancer of the Occupy movement ... They confuse acts of petty vandalism and repellent cynicism with revolution ... There is a word for this—'criminals.'"[70] During the Toronto G20 Summit in 2010, Jack Layton, the leader of Canada's left-leaning New Democratic Party, stated that "vandalism is criminal and totally unacceptable" and expressed the hope that order would be quickly restored for the sake of peaceful and respectful dialogue.[71] Once again, this is nothing new. Susan George, vice-president of ATTAC, the Association pour la taxation des transactions financières et l'aide aux citoyens (Association for the taxation of financial transactions and aid to citizens), commenting on the demonstrations against the EU in Göteborg in 2001, said that "the violence of the anarchists or vandals is more antidemocratic than the institutions they are supposedly fighting against."[72]

Voices on the far left have taken up the same refrain. The Communist Party of Canada and the Communist Party of Quebec have denounced the Black Bloc and anarchists for their "infantile foolishness" at the 2010 G20 Summit in Toronto, deriding the "childish black-bloc tactic."[73] In France, *Rouge*, the official organ of the Ligue communiste révolutionnaire (LCR), published unequivocal criticisms of the use of force during demonstrations in an article titled "'Black Bloc,' violence et intoxication." The author, Léonce Aguirre, later associated with the alter-globalization Social Forum, began by declaring that he wished to avoid "the trap of the nice demonstrators on one side and the nasty vandals on the other." Yet he then immediately launched a bald attack against the Black Blocs, arguing for an "uncompromising critique of the fantasy of a possible 'military' confrontation between a tiny minority and the state apparatus."[74]

As a sidelight to all of this, it is worth quoting the Toronto priest who, addressing his Sunday congregation the day after the massive anti-G20 demonstration, condemned "the cowardice of those who hide behind masks, whether they be white hoods or black ones."[75]

So we have come full circle, from the police officer and the politician to the communist commentator, with, along the way, the capitalist ideologue, the good protester, the spokesperson for progressive forces, the editorialist, the reporter, and the priest. All share the same sentiments and arrive at the same conclusions.

"Cancer," "idiots," "mindless thugs," "anarchists," "young bums," "devoid of political beliefs," "thirsting for violence," "vandalism," "cowardice" . . . Mere epithets under the guise of explanations? Perhaps. But words like these have very real political effects, because they rob a collective action of all credibility by reducing it to a vehicle for the supposedly brutal, irrational violence of young people.

Only one thing is missing from this unanimous chorus: the voices of those who have taken part in a Black Bloc.[76] When we listen to them, the reality becomes more complex and more interesting, and the phenomenon—its origins, dynamics, and objectives—easier to understand. I do not claim to speak on behalf of the Black Blocs; anyone acquainted with the subject knows that such a claim would be absurd. My goal, rather, is to go back to the roots of the phenomenon and examine it on the basis of Black Bloc actions, many of which I have observed firsthand,[77] communiqués (distributed primarily online),[78] and interviews with participants who have been willing to share their experiences, be it with me or with professional journalists. All told, several dozen Black Blockers active in a number of countries have spoken out in these communiqués and interviews over some 15 years, often expressing themselves in very similar terms.

After retracing the history of the Black Bloc, describing how it functions, and analyzing its political motivations, we will be able to soberly assess the shortcomings of this type of collective action and its effects on social and political mobilizations and struggles. Furthermore, we will be able to grasp more fully the political consequences of the intense criticism to which the Black Blocs have been subjected, especially the ways in which that criticism has enhanced the legitimacy of the political and social elites at the expense of anti-capitalist and antiauthoritarian protesters, thereby encouraging police repression.

CHAPTER 1

WHERE DO THE BLACK BLOCS COME FROM?

In today's liberal countries, social mobilizations feature a wide range of actions, from petitions and open letters to vigils, hunger strikes, rallies, sit-ins, blockades, sabotage, riots, and Molotov cocktail or bomb attacks. The mainstream media portray Black Bloc actions as exceptionally violent. Yet when compared to the extreme and often lethal violence prevalent in social conflicts throughout history and around the world, their actions appear restrained.

Even historical movements commonly associated with fundamental liberal rights, such as the women's suffrage movement in Britain, offer some surprises to anyone willing to give them a closer look. At the beginning of the twentieth century, Great Britain was the dominant political, military, economic, and colonial power, yet its elites were quite content to see women excluded from the electoral process (and the majority of men until 1884). In 1903, six radical women broke with the suffragists to form the Women's Social and Political Union (WSPU). Not content to simply lobby for the vote like the suffragists, the WSPU—later dubbed the "suffragettes"—undertook direct action with "Deeds, not words!" as their slogan. Within a few years, their highly effective disruptions of political party meetings would lead to women being barred from such assemblies. Undaunted, the suffragettes hid in buildings adjacent to the meeting halls and flung projectiles through the windows. They obstructed proceedings in the House of Commons and arrived unannounced at the prime minister's official residence, breaking several windows. Numerous marches to the Houses of Parliament turned into clashes with the police, which made headlines at home and abroad.[1] The suffragettes would waylay the prime minister or members of his cabinet at churches, train stations, golf courses, and so on, insulting and even pushing and slapping them. On November 21, 1911, women marched through the centre of London with hammers and stones concealed in their handbags. Along the way, they smashed the windows of the Home Office, the Local Government Board, the Exchequer, the Scottish Educational Office, Somerset House, the National Liberal Federation, the Guards' Club, two hotels, the offices of the anti-suffragist *Daily Mail* and *Daily News*, and shops including Swan and Edgar's, Lyon's, and Dunn's. More than 200 women were arrested, along with three men. A few weeks later, Emmeline Pankhurst, a suffragette leader, declared that "the argument of the broken pane of glass is the most valuable argument in modern politics."[2] Shortly afterwards, the display windows of Burberry's, Liberty's, Marshall & Snelgrove, and Kodak were shattered during a demonstration, along with the windows of some foreign companies, including Canadian Pacific. In all, 124 women were apprehended by the police. Telegraph wires between London and Glasgow were cut. Mailboxes were torched, as were post offices, train stations, warehouses, churches, private clubs, and the homes, yachts, and gardens of politicians opposed to enfranchising women. Pankhurst asserted, "We are not destroying Orchid House, breaking windows, cutting telegraph wires, injuring golf greens, in order to win the approval of the people who were attacked. If the general public were pleased with what we are doing, that would be a proof that our warfare is ineffective. We don't intend that you should be pleased."[3] More than a thousand women were jailed. Many of them undertook a hunger strike. They were force-fed and then released under the Liberal government's "Cat and Mouse Act" when they grew dangerously weak, only to be arrested again as soon as they regained their health. Once back in prison, the suffragettes resumed their hunger strike. Solidarity vigils were organized in front of the prisons, sometimes with a brass band playing. The doctor in charge of the force-feeding was jeered at and jostled in the street. Meanwhile, other suffragettes disrupted court proceedings by yelling and throwing eggs or footwear. The king was publicly heckled at formal events. In 1913, 232 arson and bomb attacks were carried out by suffragettes, and 105 more between January and August 1914, just as the First World War broke out.[4]

After the war, women finally won the right to vote, but historians are still debating whether this campaign of disruption had helped or hindered their cause. Virginia Woolf, perceptive and acerbic as ever, wrote that "English women were much criticized for using force in the battle for the franchise ... These remarks did not apply apparently to the force in the European War. The vote indeed was given to English women largely because of the help they gave to Englishmen in using force in that war."[5] True, the politicians claimed they were enfranchising women out of gratitude for their contributions to the war effort; some, however, believed this decision was motivated largely by fears of a resumption of the suffragette campaign.[6]

More recently, social movements have been known to include shock units, more or less formally organized and acknowledged as such, that are prepared to battle the police. Throughout the events of May 1968 in Paris, a number of demonstrators wore helmets and carried clubs. When the Sorbonne was occupied, the so-called Katangais could be seen circulating with weapons, including firearms. Around the same time in the United States, the Weathermen, an outgrowth of the student movement, formed units of helmeted, club-wielding protesters. In 1969, during the "Days of Rage" in Chicago, some 500 anti-racist, antiwar protesters organized in small affinity groups and equipped with motorcycle helmets, clubs, and bricks clashed head-on with the police;[7] at some of the rallies there were shock units composed entirely of women.[8] In France in the 1980s, the anti-fascist movement—in particular the network known as SCALP (Sections carrément anti-Le Pen, i.e., "utterly anti-Le Pen sections")—was known for confronting neo-Nazis.[9]

So the distinguishing feature of the Black Bloc tactic is not the recourse to force, nor is it the use of defensive and offensive gear at

A poster made in the former Sprengel chocolate factory in a working-class neighbourhood in Hannover, Germany. The neighbourhood was squatted at the time and later legalized; it remains a place for the discussion of politics and art. A play on words in German, the caption at the top of the poster—"I want Sprengel"—means both "I want Sprengel chocolates" and "I want to blast."

marches and rallies, especially since many Black Blocs have demonstrated peacefully without any such paraphernalia. Rather, what sets this tactic apart from those of other shock units is mainly its aesthetic statement—the all-black clothing in the anarcho-punk tradition—and its historical and political roots in the *Autonomen*, the "autonomous" movement of West Berlin, where the Black Bloc tactic was first deployed in the early 1980s.

The autonomous movement[10] emerged in Germany and then spread to Denmark and the Netherlands.[11] The *Autonomen's* ideological sources were diverse—Marxism, radical feminism, environmentalism, anarchism—and this ideological diversity was generally held up as a warranty of freedom. In West Germany, radical feminists had a profound effect on the *Autonomen*, injecting the movement with a more anarchist spirit than was the case elsewhere in Western Europe, where the Marxist-Leninist influence was more prevalent. The feminists sought to redefine politics by fostering autonomy on several levels: individual autonomy through the rejection of delegation, so that individuals spoke on their own behalf and not in the name of "the movement" or of all women; gender autonomy through the creation of women-only feminist collectives; decisional autonomy through the adoption of consensual decision making; and political autonomy through independence from official bodies (parties, unions, etc.) no matter how progressive. The *Autonomen* practised egalitarian and participatory politics "here and now," with neither leaders nor representatives; individual autonomy and collective autonomy were, in principle, complementary and equally important.[12]

The German autonomous groups expressed themselves politically through rent strikes and by reappropriating hundreds of buildings, which were turned into squats that served both as homes and as spaces for political activities. Many squats provided free food and clothing and housed bookstores, cafés, meeting halls, and information centres known as "infoshops," as well as concert venues and art galleries where socially committed musicians and artists could present their work.[13] The same movement occupied universities and battled with neo-Nazis who persecuted immigrants as well as with the police who protected nuclear power plants. On such occasions, the *Autonomen* would use helmets, homemade shields, clubs, and projectiles.[14]

It is not altogether clear when the term "Black Bloc" was first used. Some say it was in 1980, when a call-out for an anarchist May Day mobilization in Frankfurt asked people to "come out to the Black Bloc."[15] An alternative story dates the coinage to June 1980, after police moved to dismantle "the Free Republic of Wendland," a protest camp opposing the opening of a radioactive waste disposal site in Gorbelen, Lower Saxony. In the days that followed, solidarity rallies were organized, most notably the "Black Friday" demonstration, where it seemed as if every single person was dressed in a black leather jacket and a motorcycle helmet, face masked with a

Berlin squatters' demonstration, 1982.

A Bloc action at a 1982 squatting demo in Berlin. The German Autonomen movement was strongest during the era of squatting houses in Berlin (1980 to 1984), when a lot of people came to demonstrations dressed in black and masked up. In later years, covering one's face was forbidden by law.

In 1990 all of Mainzerstraße was squatted in Friedrichshain (East Berlin). In November 1990, 4,000 police arrived to attempt eviction. For three days thousands of people answered with barricades and militant actions.

black bandana. Subsequent German media reports referred to the *Schwarzer Block* (i.e., the Black Bloc).[16] Still others maintain that the term was coined in December 1980 by the West Berlin police. Having decided to put an end to the squats, city authorities had permitted the police to carry out a series of extremely forceful evictions. Faced with the imminent threat of a brutal police action, a number of *Autonomen* wearing black masks and clothes went into the street to defend their squats. Against this backdrop, a trial was held that focused on a "criminal organization" known as the "the Black Bloc." But the prosecution's case collapsed, with the authorities admitting that the organization never existed.[17] Then in 1981 a pamphlet titled "Schwarzer Block" appeared, with the following explanation: "There are no programs, no statutes, and no members of the Black Block.

There are, however, political ideas and utopias, which determine our lives and our resistance. This resistance has many names, and one of them is the Black Bloc."[18]

A massive Black Bloc was formed in Hamburg in 1986 to defend the Hafenstrasse squat. Some 1,500 Black Blockers, supported by 10,000 other demonstrators, confronted the police and saved the squat. "It was a great victory," said an activist in the autonomous movement, "proving it was possible to prevent evictions."[19] The street mobilization took place in tandem with clandestine actions against the threats of eviction and assaults by the police: small groups torched a dozen shops, the homes of certain politicians, and some municipal buildings. Black Blocs also appeared at rallies organized against US President Ronald Reagan's visit to West Berlin in June 1987. And when the World Bank and the International Monetary Fund (IMF) met in September 1988, again in West Berlin, a Black Bloc took part in the protests.[20] In some protests, some *Autonomen* wearing black hoods walked naked in the streets, offering the paradoxical spectacle of a highly vulnerable Black Bloc.

Today, Germany has the largest Black Blocs (often referred to as "autonomous Blocs" instead of "Black Blocs"). The country's security service, the Office for the Protection of the Constitution, estimates—no doubt a little too accurately—that Germany's Black Blockers number around 5,800.[21] At the yearly May Day anti-capitalist rallies in Berlin, Black Blocs bring together between 2,000 and 4,000 people dressed entirely in black, encircled by banners and wearing black hoodies (leather jackets are no longer fashionable) and dark glasses (now that masks have been outlawed in Germany). These demonstrations have become so popular among European militant networks that many *Autonomen* complain about the "activist tourists" who seek out riots as opportunities to carouse, are indifferent to local realities, and, worst of all, leave town as abruptly as they had come. Indeed, it is not uncommon for such individuals to buy beer along the demonstration route and fling the empties at the police, only to be berated or even manhandled by "straightedge" (i.e., no tobacco, alcohol, or drugs) *Autonomen,* who may smash their bottles and impress on them that politics is serious

Thousands demonstrated when US President Ronald Reagan visited Berlin in 1982. At Nollendorfplatz in Berlin-Schöneberg, police encircled the protesters with razor wire. The demonstrators tried to escape, answering with stones and other militant actions.

business. Even so, in 2013 in the Kreutzberg district of Berlin, posters in English—hence, aimed at activist tourists—invited people to join an "Anarchist/Autonomous Block."

Various other occasions arise in Germany for forming Black Blocs. For example, on February 11, to confront neo-Nazis gathering in Dresden to commemorate the carpet bombing of the city during the Second World War. Because of the size and dynamism of the German autonomous movement, a variety of networks can simultaneously send out calls for the formation of several autonomous blocs. The blocs stemming from the "anti-fascist action" network are composed largely of men, and their attitude is more macho. Women form the majority in anti-racist networks, where issues of diversity and inclusion are of greater concern.

In recent years there have been calls for "multicolour blocs," on the grounds that it may be culturally insensitive to associate "black" with anonymity and the use of force. One such call was sent out on April 1, 2012, for a rally in Eisenach against a meeting of nationalist "fraternities." The poster showed two characters clothed in the Black Bloc style, except that one wore purple and the other pink. Despite this, most of the participants came wearing black, and a few of the anti-fascists even made homophobic and sexist remarks about their more flamboyantly dressed comrades. At the No Border camp, held in Stockholm in June 2012 primarily to denounce the homophobic and sexist elements of European immigration policy, a call was sent out once again for a multicolour bloc but was heeded by only a handful of Swedish and German activists.

It is also worth noting the emergence in the 2000s of extreme-right "autonomous-nationalist" or "anti-antifascist action" groups, which appropriate the Black Bloc style when marching in neo-Nazi demonstrations: dark glasses, hoods, banners all around, electro music. Autonomous-nationalist blocs like these have assembled as many as a thousand fascists at major rallies.[22]

How did the Black Bloc tactic migrate from West Berlin in the 1980s to Seattle in 1999? The sociologists Charles Tilly, Doug McAdam, and Dieter Rucht, who specialize in social movements, have shown that for different periods and places there exist repertoires of collective actions deemed effective and legitimate for the defence and promotion of a cause.[23] These repertoires are transformed and disseminated over time and across borders from one social movement to another, in accordance with the experiences of militants and changes in the political sphere. The Black Bloc tactic was disseminated in the 1990s mainly through the punk and far left or ultra-left counterculture via fanzines, touring punk music groups, and the personal contacts of travelling activists. In North America, the Black Bloc tactic is believed to have emerged for the first time in January 1991 during a rally in Washington denouncing the first Iraq War. The World Bank building was targeted, and windows were smashed. A Black Bloc was organized later the same year in San Francisco at a Columbus Day rally denouncing 500 years of genocide

*A poster calling—
in English—for an
"Anarchist/Autonomous
block" at the 2013 May
Day demonstration
in Berlin.*

perpetrated against First Nations, and another appeared at the march in Washington for the right of women to control their own bodies. Anarchist journals such as *Love and Rage* then helped make the Black Bloc tactic known throughout the American anarchist community.[24]

The tactic was also taken up in the early 1990s by members of Anti-Racist Action (ARA), an anti-authoritarian, anti-racist movement in the United States and Canada that focused on direct confrontation with neo-Nazis and White Supremacists. Activists from the Toronto section of the ARA travelled to Montreal on September 22, 1993, where they assembled a small Black Bloc at a rally protesting a meeting— eventually cancelled—where two French mayors belonging to the National Front were to be the guest speakers. The upshot was a tense face-off with the police, a volley of paint bombs aimed at the restaurant that had welcomed the Frontists, and a chase through the streets as

Göttingen protest poster made by kuk ("Kunst und Kampf" or "Art and Struggle"), the "Art Division" of Antifa M. At the time, this poster style was quite modern and highly influential. The main text reads: "Protest against Fascism and Police Terrorism," with the slogan at the bottom: "Together, the future belongs to us." Göttingen, Germany c. 1989.

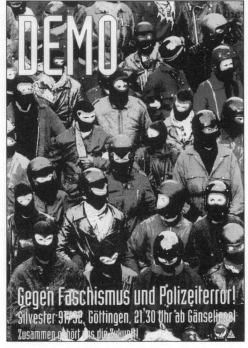

demonstrators drove away some 30 neo-Nazi skinheads who had come to protect the venue. On April 24, 1999, a Black Bloc about 1,500 strong took part in a march in Philadelphia demanding the release of Mumia Abu-Jamal, a founder of the local Black Panther branch, who had been accused of killing a police officer in 1981 and sentenced to death.

Alter-Globalization

But it was on November 30, 1999, during the demonstrations against the WTO meeting in Seattle, that the media broadcast the image of the Black Bloc around the world. Police in the United States had used pepper spray and mass arrests during the 1990s against non-violent demonstrators at a series of civil disobedience actions launched by radical West Coast environmentalists. On the assumption that they would take the same course of action again, the Black Blockers opted for a mobile tactic that would prevent large-scale arrests and pepper-spray and tear gas injuries.[25] On the morning of November 30, 1999, the police thoroughly doused with pepper spray and tear gas groups of non-violent activists who since 7 a.m. had been blocking the entrance to the convention centre, and tear gas supplies were running low. At 11 a.m. the Black Bloc went into action in an area far from the convention centre. The Black Bloc shattered the windows of some banks and international firms, then vanished before the police could react.

There was extensive media coverage of the Black Bloc in Seattle, and this helped disseminate its distinctive features—black clothing, face masks, and strikes against symbolic economic and political targets. The mainstream media took a rather negative view of Black Blocs; the debate about their activities was more nuanced in the alternative media, especially on the independent online network Indymedia, where one could read Black Bloc communiqués and view photos and videos of them in action.[26] Fascinated by such images, and won over by arguments defending the legitimacy and effectiveness of the Black Bloc tactic, some individuals came to identify with this type of action and decided to organize their own Black Blocs at the first opportunity—for example, when a major international summit was announced for their city.

In fact, the Seattle protest was part of a vast transnational social movement—variously referred to as the anti-globalization or "alter-globalization" movement or the "movement of movements"—that takes advantage of the summits held by the WTO, the IMF, the G8 and G20, the EU, and so on, to organize several days of conferences and actions in or near the host city. This broad and heterogeneous movement expresses itself through diverse street-level actions. The major social democratic organizations (labour unions, farmers' unions, feminist federations, left-wing political parties, and so forth) hold a "unitary" march supervised by a sturdy corps of marshals. Meanwhile, various militant groups carry out a number of disruptive actions. Black Blocs are organized on such occasions, often marching peacefully but ready to resort to physical force, depending on the context and their relative strength. Black Blocs have also been involved in mobilizations not

Photograph by Michael Kappel. Reproduced by permission of the photographer.

Black Blockers and Occupy activists at a demonstration during the Chicago NATO Summit, May 20, 2012.

directly connected with the alter-globalization movement; this was the case at the 2002 and 2009 NATO summits in Prague and Strasbourg respectively, and at the Republican Party Convention in New York in August and September 2004.

The Black Bloc tactic can acquire a specific meaning, one that varies with the local cultural context. For instance, in Mexico in the 1990s, anarcho-punks were especially attracted to Black Bloc aesthetics, in particular, the wearing of masks, as this was also a feature of the Zapatista Army of National Liberation, even though the anarcho-punks' relationship with the Zapatistas was ambivalent.[27]

Behind the Masks

It is difficult to draw a precise sociological profile of the men and women who participate in Black Blocs, not just because they wear disguises, but also because no two Black Blocs are the same. While I am well aware that Black Blocs are neither homogeneous nor all alike, my own observations indicate that they are often composed mainly of young people (though some members may be over 50) and men (in some instances, only 5 percent of Black Blockers are women).[28] Even in Western anti-fascist and anti-racist networks, Black Bloc members are overwhelmingly of European extraction, to the virtual exclusion of people of colour.[29] While this can also be said of many political networks on the left, the direct actions specific to Black Blocs may give rise to an additional factor—immigrants and people of colour are at greater risk when faced with repression.[30]

The French sociologist Geoffrey Pleyers has identified both thrill-seeking youths with low levels of political awareness and highly politicized activists among Black Bloc participants.[31] It is true that some individuals join a Black Bloc under the influence of their friends or out of conformism or a simple desire to vent repressed rage, but no one can force another to adopt this tactic, which is based on respecting the autonomy of all those taking part in it.

Not all Black Bloc participants are self-declared anarchists. In Egypt, for instance, they may be political activists, or Ultra (soccer) fans or Heavy Metal fans. However, one commentator notes that "Tahrir itself [i.e., the main public square in Cairo, occupied in January 2013 for weeks by thousands opposing the new Muslim Brotherhood government] remains in many ways the epitome of the ideas of horizontalism and self-organization that are at the core of modern anarchist theory and practice."[32]

In their communiqués, manifestos, and interviews, many Black Blocs have underscored the diversity of their membership. In "Letter From Inside the Black Bloc," for example, published a few days after the demonstrations protesting the 2001 G8 Summit in Genoa, Mary Black wrote:

> Most folks I know who have used Black Bloc tactics have day jobs working for nonprofits. Some are schoolteachers, labor organizers, or students. Some don't have full-time jobs, but instead spend most of their time working for change in their communities. They start urban garden projects and bike libraries; they cook food for

Food Not Bombs and other groups. These are thinking and caring folks who, if they did not have radical political and social agendas, would be compared with nuns, monks, and others who live their lives in service. There is a fair amount of diversity in who we are and what we believe. I've known folks in the Black Bloc who come from as far south as Mexico City and as far north as Montreal. I think that the stereotype is correct that we are mostly young and mostly white, although I wouldn't agree that we are mostly men. When I'm dressed from head to toe in baggy black clothes, and my face is covered up, most people think I'm a man too. The behavior of Black Bloc protesters is not associated with women, so reporters often assume we are all guys.[33]

Accounts like this are apparently motivated by a wish to accurately portray Black Bloc members and in so doing to counter accusations that they are nothing but young delinquents with no political awareness. Self-representations like these give the lie to an all too frequent criticism of Black Blocs: that it is impossible for an activist to do two things at once or even one after the other—that is, take part in a riot and also organize within global or local movements that help exploited and marginalized people.[34]

Statements like Mary Black's are also legitimizing moves, similar to one made in 2011 after an "anti-cuts" rally in London, when a Black Bloc participant identifying himself as a "low-paid public sector worker" told a *Guardian* reporter: "We saw plenty of nurses, education workers, tech workers, unemployed workers, students, campaigners and charity workers on the bloc."[35] Another stated:

You would be incredibly surprised by the demographic that uses black bloc tactics, in terms of age, gender, occupation. The media like to paint a picture of hooligans and thugs, mindless men on the rampage. It is simply not true. There are women and probably transgender people too. Some of the scariest-looking anarchists work in jobs like social care and mental health. It doesn't come from a thuggish place.[36]

Unexpectedly, the group portrait that emerges is one of responsible and reasonable citizens of both sexes.

During the Quebec student strike of 2012, the mainstream media inveighed against the supposed infiltration of student demonstrations by Black Blocs. Here is how a group of "anarchists among many" responded to this claim in their "Manifeste du Carré noir" (Black Square Manifesto):

> We are women and men. We are students. We are workers. We are unemployed. We are angry. We are not co-opting a strike. We have been part of the movement from the beginning, one of its facets, on a par with all the others ... We do not infiltrate demonstrations, we help organize them, we bring them to life. We are not sabotaging the strike, we are an integral part of it, we help organize it, we make its heart beat.[37]

Many of the people I interviewed were or had been social science students (such encounters were no doubt attributable in part to my own academic background). In a number of cases, their research projects dealt with the political significance and consequences of demonstrations and direct actions, which suggests that their political involvement was grounded in serious political thinking. According to the communiqué put out by the Seattle Black Bloc in 1999, the majority of its members "have been studying the effects of the global economy, genetic engineering, resource extraction, transportation, labor practices, elimination of indigenous autonomy, animal rights and human rights and we've done activism on these issues for many years. We are neither ill-informed nor unexperienced."[38] Most of the individuals I interviewed about the Black Blocs were seasoned activists or were active in various community or political organizations (opposed to neo-Nazis, racism, police brutality, and so on), or they helped produce political newspapers.[39] It bears repeating, however, that there is no uniform profile of the militants behind the black masks. A punk music fan does not necessarily participate in a Black Bloc; conversely, a Black Blocker may dislike punk music—or, for that matter, university.

Many Black Blockers say that their use of force is the result of a political assessment based on their personal involvement in non-violent actions that they came to see as inadequate at best.[40] One veteran militant who had joined various Black Blocs told me: "The men and women I know who have taken part in a Black Bloc are all activists, some of them quite experienced. They are somehow disillusioned because they've concluded that peaceful methods are too limited and play into the hands of the powers that be. So to stop being victims, they decide to use violence."[41]

Internal Organization

It is possible that some Black Blocs are only gatherings of individuals who are content to march as a group in a demonstration or who take advantage of the relative anonymity afforded by their attire to carry out certain direct actions more or less randomly. In other words, a Black Bloc is not necessarily endowed with real, collective decision-making power.

Like all anarchist groups, a Black Bloc attempts to function on an egalitarian and libertarian basis, without a hierarchy or any positions of authority. Whenever deliberation is possible, decisions are made collectively; each member can submit proposals and discuss those put forward by others. Consensus is considered preferable to voting, which is rare. The affinity group structure facilitates autonomous and prompt decision making. The "affinity group" is a form of organization rooted in the Spanish anarchist tradition.[42] From the moment it was founded in 1927, the Federación Anarquista Ibérica (FAI, Iberian Anarchist Federation) operated through *grupos de afinidad*. Since then, this principle has been embraced by diverse political movements, including pacifists, feminists, and AIDS activists (those of Act Up! in particular). An affinity group is generally composed of between a half-dozen and several dozen individuals whose affinity results from ties that bind them, such as belonging to the same school, workplace, or political organization. Situated where friendship and political solidarity intersect, an affinity group can be thought of as a circle of "amilitants" who respect and trust one another. The coinage "amilitant" is used here to signify both the importance of friendship (*ami* is French for "friend") and the negation (indicated by the prefix *a-*) of the traditional image of the militant—that is, one whose actions and identity are largely determined by organizational allegiance. The concept of "amilitancy" is in tune with the political mindset of the many contemporary anti-authoritarian activists who are unfamiliar with or opposed to traditional militancy, with its heavy emphasis on loyalty to the organization—party, union, and such—and its penchant for authoritarian structures and hierarchies based on participation and political experience.

The primacy of friendship in affinity groups is conducive to egalitarian, deliberative, and consensual decision making. It also facilitates the voluntary division of all tasks within and among affinity groups. A female member of the Black Bloc in Toronto in 2010 noted that, given the confusion and high level of tension prevailing when an action or a riot is under way, co-ordination is easier *within* an affinity group than *between* such groups.[43] Before a demonstration, taking into account the political context and the experience and disposition of each individual, the amilitants agree on what exactly they will be doing in the Black Bloc.

A woman who participated in several Black Blocs in Quebec said that this form of organization provides "a place, a safe space where individuals can gather, where they feel safer because people help each other and other people are helping behind the front lines. Some are alive to the call of the brick, others prefer to protect the group, especially by watching out for police infiltrators, media representatives, and peace-police."[44]

Careful consideration is also given to the potential consequences of being arrested for someone with vulnerable immigration status, family responsibilities, health problems, or a record of previous arrests, or who faces other issues. Individuals deemed "unarrestable" may volunteer for low-risk tasks, which can involve staying away from the action. Those amilitants who prefer not to engage in street actions may form affinity groups in charge of legal support in the event of arrests, or responsible for transportation, lodging, water and food supplies, media contacts, psychological support, and so on.

Some groups may choose to engage in offensive actions and accordingly arm themselves with clubs, slingshots, billiard balls, even

Molotov cocktails. For defensive actions, the equipment includes shields, chest protectors, gloves, shin guards, helmets, and gas masks. Some will carry out reconnaissance and communications operations using bicycles and walkie-talkies or cellphones. Others will act as medics, bringing relief to tear gas or pepper spray victims and administering first aid to the injured. Still others will maintain group morale with music and songs. A number of activists may simply join the Black Bloc in the street, wearing black clothes and masks, with no specific equipment or task but ready to improvise according to how the demonstration unfolds. Finally, the affinity group structure and the small size of certain Black Blocs enables activists to hold deliberative meetings minutes before the demonstration—as they did in Calgary during the mobilization against the Kananaskis G8 Summit in June 2002—or even in the middle of a demonstration, as was the case during the marches against the G8 Summit in Évian in June 2003.

One participant in the blocking actions in Annemasse—part of the mobilization against the 2003 G8 Summit—who herself engaged only in non-violent civil disobedience, offered this analysis of the political dynamics among the protesters:

> I found it extraordinary that we could hold delegates' meetings right in the middle of the blocking action. There were barricades, fires had been lit, the police were slinging a lot of tear gas. And still, a meeting was called, with someone yelling, "meeting in ten minutes near the road sign." The meeting took place barely a few hundred metres from where the police stood, and it allowed us to decide on our course of action ... Everyone had the chance to inform the others of what the needs were: "We need reinforcements against the police," "we need help building the barricades," "we should send people out to scouting...," etc. ... So we were able to act dynamically in the midst of the action without just one person shouting "we must do this or that!" ... The police officers see you as a crowd and assume you're going to act like a crowd. The affinity group model disrupts that dynamic: you don't act like a crowd anymore but like a rational being. Affinity groups help us realize

*Molotov cocktails are made before a general strike in Athens,
May 5, 2010.*

our own power. The police are still surprised and baffled by affinity groups. They're thinking, "we have water canons, tear gas, but here are these people who are supposed to run away, holding a meeting to decide what they're going to do!"[45]

In sum, Black Blocs function according to principles associated with the anarchist political tradition, such as freedom and equality. These principles are embodied in procedures and practices such as general assemblies and horizontal, non-hierarchical structures. This approach answers not just political but also moral needs. It can also be highly effective on the ground, making it possible—in principle—to transform an apparently irrational throng into a rational political actor aware of its choices and of the significance of its acts.

In practice, though, affinity groups do not preclude—any more than formal hierarchical structures do—informal power games based on the charisma, experience, and skills of individual members or on their symbolic, cultural, and economic assets. However, unlike the situation in hierarchical organizations, people in an affinity group or a Black Bloc cannot use their informal power to acquire positions of vested authority through which they might augment their informal power with the formal variety. Allowing that informal leaders arise in all human groups,[46] Black Blocs have no "chiefs" whose official position would enable them to impose their will on "subordinates." In addition, since Black Blocs are ephemeral, there are limited opportunities for any person to develop self-interested influence within the group.

Some Black Blocs or component groups involve little or no formal, co-ordinated organization. At some demonstrations, for instance, individuals come to the gathering place in masks and black clothes and spontaneously set up a Black Bloc—that is, a group marching together as a compact unit—without any prior collective decision making. At times of direct action, one or more individuals may decide to act alone—to graffiti a wall or hurl projectiles at a window or the police—without consulting other members of the Black Bloc.

Tactical Diversity

On November 30, 1999, in Seattle, the Black Bloc targeted symbols of capitalism—bank branches and the retail outlets of large multinationals—in the city's shopping district, far from the activists blocking the entrance to the WTO meeting. A subsequent Black Bloc communiqué listed some of these targets along with their political significance:

> Fidelity Investment (major investor in Occidental Petroleum, the bane of the U'wa tribe in Columbia), Bank of America, US Bancorp, Key Bank and Washington Mutual Bank (financial institutions key in the expansion of corporate repression), Old Navy, Banana Republic and the GAP (as Fisher family businesses, rapers of Northwest forest lands and sweatshop laborers), NikeTown and Levi's (whose overpriced products are made in sweatshops), McDonald's (slave-wage fast-food peddlers responsible for destruction of tropical rainforests for grazing land and slaughter of animals), Starbucks

(peddlers of an addictive substance whose products are harvested at below-poverty wages by farmers who are forced to destroy their own forests in the process), Warner Bros. (media monopolists), Planet Hollywood (for being Planet Hollywood).[47]

The Canadian sociologist and activist Lesley J. Wood and other observers of direct actions have explained that the target is the message.[48] In other words, what renders such an action intelligible is its target.

Because Black Blocs are autonomous, each being composed of different people acting in different circumstances, they do not always choose the same targets, nor do they always resort to force in demonstrations. In April 2000, during the marches in Washington against the IMF and World Bank, the Black Bloc focused its efforts on protecting non-violent protesters under attack from the police. When the IMF and World Bank held a joint meeting in Prague in September of that year, a Black Bloc attempted unsuccessfully to force its way to the convention centre, confronting a police barricade head-on with clubs, stones, and Molotov cocktails. A month later in Montreal, in the wake of a rally against a G20 Summit, a very small Black Bloc drew a barrage of criticism because its members had flung various objects at the police from a position behind other protesters, a number of whom were hit by the projectiles and in some cases had their clothes stained by paint bombs. A Black Blocker testified to the same problem in the protest against the NATO Summit in Strasbourg in 2009.[49]

In 2001 in Buffalo, a Black Bloc entered a poor neighbourhood and collected the garbage. When bewildered reporters asked what they were doing, they explained: "You wrote that we would trash the town. We decided to pick up the trash!"[50] Also in 2001, during the Free Trade Area of the Americas (FTAA) negotiations in Quebec City, several small Black Blocs stormed the security perimeter and fought with the police protecting it; but they also shielded other demonstrators from charging riot police. Elsewhere, Black Blocs have demonstrated peacefully, as on April 22, 2001, at the rallies in Washington for women's rights.

Paul, a veteran of demonstrations in Europe, summed up the thinking that goes on in a Black Bloc before a decision is made on whether or not to use force: "First, the purpose of the rally, the political motivation behind it. Next, the general situation of the political or social movement, the size of the crowd, its composition, the people you see in it. It's a gut feeling. You know from experience when a demonstration is going to get out of hand or, in different circumstances, that it would be better for it not to." Referring to the July 19, 2001, rally in Genoa during the G8 Summit, where the demand was for freedom of movement and regularized status for political asylum seekers, Paul remarked that the demonstration stayed peaceful even though 1,000 people with masks were bringing up the rear. Peace was maintained because everyone knew "it was too dangerous for [the illegal refugees]. You can afford to spend the night in jail, but they can't."[51]

Another Black Bloc marched peacefully in a demonstration in Calgary in June 2002, during the G8 Summit in Kananaskis. Once again, this behaviour was the outcome of rational political choices. The previous day, a general meeting had determined that the first part of the march would be non-violent and that only during the second part would the use of force be acceptable. Midway through the demonstration, the Black Blockers deliberated and, recognizing their unfavourable position vis-à-vis the police, decided to continue to march peacefully through the streets of Calgary.

On November 21, 2002, 3,000 anarcho-communists demonstrated at the NATO Summit in Prague, where the military presence was overwhelming. Using force would have placed the demonstrators in a very hazardous situation due to their relative weakness. At one point, a police car wended its way into the march, heightening tensions. Sensing a provocation, the Black Bloc moved in to protect the vehicle from attacks, which would have prompted a brutal police response.

By contrast, during the G8 Summit in Évian, when not the slightest demonstration was under way, a Black Bloc of 100 individuals swarmed into Geneva's central shopping district on the evening of Saturday, May 31, 2003, when all was quiet, smashing windows, lobbing Molotov cocktails, and vanishing after a few minutes. Over the following days, Black Blocs took part in blocking actions in co-ordination with other groups of demonstrators.

Then in June 2003, during the protests in Thessaloniki against the EU summit, Black Blockers split into two groups: those advocating a concentrated attack against the police, and those in favour of striking at symbols of capitalism in the city centre. In the end, the Black Bloc confronted the police on the first day of demonstrations and targeted symbols of capitalism on the second (while skirmishing with police officers endeavouring to protect private property).

In Miami in November 2003, during a protest against high-level discussions on the Free Trade Area of the Americas, the Black Bloc tried in vain to protect some giant puppets from the police, who spent 30 minutes destroying them after the routed demonstrators had abandoned them on Seaside Plaza.[52] At the major unitary rally protesting the Republican Party Convention in New York in August 2004, Black Blockers marched without masks until the demonstration reached the convention venue, at which point they donned their masks and burned a giant puppet representing a dragon. The ensuing battle with the police lasted an hour. In June 2005, during the G8 Summit in Scotland, a Black Bloc undertook a "Suicide March," which got under way before dawn, leaving the protesters' temporary, self-managed camp to draw police away from the many affinity groups that were deploying throughout the countryside to obstruct the highways at sunrise. After confronting several police barricades with clubs and stones and damaging property belonging to multinational corporations, the Suicide March reached a highway and blocked it.

Those are only a few examples of Black Blocs in recent years. This historical sketch amply illustrates the diversity of Black Bloc tactical choices, which often include marching alongside other protesters without engaging in any unconventional actions.

Other Blocs

Large demonstrations and mobilizations can encompass a wide variety of practices: carrying banners, flags, and placards, playing musical instruments, wearing masks and costumes, and so on. Also, unions and other participating organizations encourage their members to march together behind their official banners, and supply them with placards, T-shirts, and the like so as to heighten their visibility and sense of collective identity. And for those who favour confrontation but do not feel in tune with the Black Blocs, there are other types of "blocs."

The Red Blocs are made up of communists from an assortment of groups. They typically carry red flags bearing the hammer and sickle, at times with the portrait of Che Guevara or Mao Zedong, and follow their leaders' orders. Unlike Black Blocs with their affinity groups, Red Blocs have an authoritarian and hierarchical structure. *Socialisme Maintenant!*, a French-language periodical (last published in April 2002) of the Revolutionary Communist Party of Canada, disseminated instructions on how to form a "red fist," a sort of affinity group composed of "five comrades" entrusted with a specific task during a demonstration: holding a banner, distributing leaflets and newspapers, or carrying out attacks against the police or symbolic targets. "The red fist," these instructions added, "does not determine on its own the task to which it will devote itself."[53]

The "White Bloc," also known as the Tute Bianche (White Overalls), originated in the Italian social centres—that is, political squats—and remain very close to Communist Youth organizations, unemployed workers' movements, and the Zapatistas of Chiapas. Their white uniforms provide anonymity, just as black clothing does for the Black Blocs. Being advocates of offensive non-violence, the Tute Bianche wear makeshift armour (foam rubber mattresses, helmets, gloves, masks, leg protectors) and advance with their arms linked, using the collective mass of their bodies to crash through police lines, occasionally throwing inner tubes as well. One political goal of the Tute Bianche is to overturn the dynamic whereby the media systematically blame the protesters whenever a demonstration gets out of hand. They therefore take great pains to ensure that the media have a clear view of their obviously defensive equipment. A Tute Bianche militant explains it this way:

> We wanted people to understand on which side lay reason, and
> which had started the violence ... People can see images on the
> TV news that can't be manipulated: a mountain of bodies that

advances, seeking the least harm possible to itself, against the violent defenders of an order that produces wars and misery. And the results are visible, people understand this, the journalists can't invent lies that contradict the images; last but not least, the batons bounce off the padding.[54]

The Tute Bianche first went into action in Prague in September 2000, but their most important battle took place in Genoa during the G8 Summit in July 2001. Representatives of the Tute Bianche invited reporters to attend their training session at the Carlini Stadium, where they mobilized between 15,000 and 20,000 people, who then marched on the security fence, massed behind protective Plexiglas panels mounted on wheels. In short order, the contingent was viciously attacked by the police. Some demonstrators chose to disperse, while others preferred to stand and fight. Similar groups have been created in Australia, Spain, Finland, and Great Britain.[55] However, since the failed action of 2001 in Genoa, this tactic has seldom been deployed.

In addition to the Black Blocs and the Tute Bianche, there is a third type of bloc, variously referred to as Pink Blocs, Pink and Silver Blocs, or Carnival Blocs. These bring together activists whose goal is to meld politics, art, and pleasure in a single action. They don zany, carnivalesque costumes and enjoy blurring the boundaries of sexual identity.[56] Various tasks are taken on by different affinity groups: street theatre and giant puppet shows, samba band performances, first aid, and so on. The Pink Blocs originated in Reclaim the Streets, a British group known for its anti-capitalist carnivals, and Rhythms of Resistance, a militant percussion group whose mobile, offensive approach has brought them into direct contact with police lines.[57] The Pink Bloc first made itself conspicuous in Prague in September 2000, when it succeeded in outflanking the police and came close enough to the convention centre to force its evacuation and thus curtail a meeting of the IMF and the World Bank. In the United States, at the 2000 Republican and Democratic conventions, members of the group Billionaires for Bush and Gore dressed up in formal attire and handed out phony banknotes to the police to thank them for cracking down on dissidents. The

A participant in a Pink & Black Bloc surveys her surround-
ings at the National Equality March in Washington, DC,
October 11, 2009.

police, meanwhile, were left bewildered by members of the revolutionary anarchist Clowns Bloc, who from atop their high-wheeled bicycles
gave the Billionaires for Bush and Gore a (very limp) drubbing![58]

During the EU Summit in Göteborg in June 2001, the British prime
minister Tony Blair referred to the protest movement that was making
itself heard in the streets as an "anarchist travelling circus."[59] Activists
in London appropriated Blair's gibe, reproducing it on a banner for
their May Day rallies; others have taken it more literally and formed
clown armies. The oldest such army is that of the Christiana squat in
Copenhagen, while the one that has recently attracted the most attention is the Clandestine Insurgent Rebel Clown Army of Great Britain,
which first deployed during the 2005 G8 Summit in Scotland.[60] To
quote from the Clown Army's own statement: "We are clowns because

Black Blockers attempt to lure the police with donuts strung as if on fishing rods during the Quebec student strike, Montreal, 2012.

what else can one be in such a stupid world. Because inside everyone is a lawless clown trying to escape. Because nothing undermines authority like holding it up to ridicule." The statement continues: "We are an army because we live on a planet in permanent war—a war of money against life, of profit against dignity, of progress against the future … Because only an army can declare absurd war on absurd war."[61] Though they practise disruptive direct action, the clowns are averse to using force, which nevertheless did not prevent them from joining in the highway blocking actions that were part of the mobilization against the G8 Summit in Scotland.[62] Rebel clowns were also active at the NATO summit in Strasbourg in 2009.

Although more rare, Book Blocs were formed during the 2010 student mobilizations in Italy and later by protesters in Great Britain and Oakland. This action involved establishing a line of defence during a demonstration using handmade shields in the shape of books, with the titles (*Don Quixote*, *1984*, *The Possessed*, *Moby Dick*) and sometimes the authors' names visible on the front.[63] In front-line confrontations with the police, Book Blockers have worn helmets as well.

In sum, the various militant tactics, though not always in harmony with one another, contribute to the idea of tactical diversity. The boundaries between the different blocs are porous, which allows for hybrid experiences. In 2005 in Scotland, the Black Bloc, as previously mentioned, took part in a Suicide March to divert the police's attention from the battalions of clowns and their allies that had scattered into the woods, re-emerging later throughout the countryside to block the highways. Later, the clowns surrounded the police who had encircled the Black Bloc, ridiculing and distracting them.[64] During the 2003 G8 Summit in Évian, a 1,500-strong Pink Bloc co-ordinated its blocking actions in Lausanne with a Black Bloc of 500 individuals.[65] In November 2001, during the joint meeting of the IMF and the World Bank in Ottawa, the environmentalist collective Living River, which practises pagan rituals in demonstrations and counts the feminist Starhawk among its members, formed a solidarity circle around a Black Bloc to protect it from the police. Waving scarves, the boisterous band stepped in between the police and the Black Bloc, allowing the latter to slip away.[66]

The contours of the blocs are sometimes hazy. In Montreal on March 7, 2004, during a "unitary" International Women's Day march, the Pink Panthers, a queer affinity group, organized a Pink Bloc whose participants, male and female alike, wore brightly coloured clothes and pink masks.[67] Despite the marshals' attempts to intimidate them, they succeeded in staging a kiss-in in front of the rostrum to attest to the queer element within the women's movement. The "maNUfestations" that took place during the 2012 Quebec student strike saw hundreds of women and men marching half-naked; some of the women's faces were hidden behind black masks (as had been those of naked squatters protesting in Berlin, in the 1980s) so that they could walk in the streets at once nude and incognito, in an improbable Black Bloc incarnating both force and vulnerability.

. . .

Finally, Black Blocs are far from alone in sometimes resorting to force during demonstrations. Indeed, they often find themselves amid a welter of affinity groups and individuals that are attacking symbolic targets, or flinging tear gas canisters back at the police and showering them with projectiles.

There are also individuals, alone or in affinity groups, who choose to make their political opinions known through the use of force, but without wearing black. For example, to protest against the December 2000 meeting of EU heads of state in Nice, demonstrators assailed businesses and banks and confronted the police without forming a Black Bloc. In Quebec City in April 2001, very few of the people who took down a section of the security fence were dressed in black. And during the 2012 student strike in Quebec, Black Blocs sometimes went into action simultaneously with other people who, though not identifiable as Black Blockers, also stood up to the police. With the other protesters, the Black Bloc formed a line of confrontation and hurled rocks at the police. That is what happened at the riot that erupted when the Quebec Liberal Party held its convention in Victoriaville. During the same student strike, small groups in Black Bloc attire demonstrated in Montreal waving the Quebec flag, denoting nationalist sentiments at variance with the anarchist ideology generally associated with the Black Blocs.

Moreover, women and men who come to demonstrations with the firm intention of marching peacefully may decide to use force after witnessing police violence or experiencing it themselves. Sociologists studying the interaction between demonstrators and police officers have repeatedly observed and analyzed the provocative effect of police actions.[68] This effect appears to have been at work a number of times in recent years, the events in Genoa being the most dramatic case in point. There, a vast number of initially non-violent demonstrators ended up responding to the indiscriminate violence of repressive forces.

The Black Blocs and their allies adapt their actions to the immediate situation and keep their options open, based on the political sensibilities, reasoning, and experience of each individual regarding the appropriate means for expressing political convictions.[69]

CHAPTER 2

POLITICAL VIOLENCE

VIOLENCE means working for 40 years, getting miserable wages and
    wondering if you ever get to retire . . .

VIOLENCE means state bonds, robbed pension funds and the stock-
    market fraud . . .

VIOLENCE means unemployment, temporary employment . . .

VIOLENCE means work "accidents" . . .

VIOLENCE means being driven sick because of hard work . . .

VIOLENCE means consuming psych-drugs and vitamins in order to cope
    with exhausting working hours . . .

VIOLENCE means working for money to buy medicines in order to fix your
    labor power commodity . . .

VIOLENCE means dying on ready-made beds in horrible hospitals, when you
    can't afford bribing.

      —Proletarians from the occupied headquarters of the General
        Confederation of Greek Workers (GSEE), Athens, December 2008

All ideologies and, for that matter, religions have found ways to justify and encourage the violence of their followers whenever it has been considered necessary, so it should not surprise us that anarchists and Black Bloc members have sometimes employed force to defend and further their ideas. Liberalism, national-ism, Marxism-Leninism, fascism, and Christianity, each in its own way, and far more frequently than anarchism, have all resorted to assassination, often of anarchists. Hence, the association of the terms "anarchism" and "anarchist" with chaos and bloody violence has always been questionable, especially because not every anarchist supports the use of force; indeed, some adhere to *non*-violence, at times dogmatically.[1]

A case in point is the somewhat surrealistic debate on the distinction between violence and non-violence that took place among Boston anarchists in 1978. The anti-nuclear organization Clamshell Alliance was planning a massive occupation of the Seabrook Nuclear Power Plant construction site about 50 kilometres from Boston. After the initial occupation in April 1977, when 1,414 activists were arrested, a steel fence had been erected around the site, and the anarchist affinity group Hard Rain proposed bringing bolt cutters to open a breach in the barrier. A number of activists opposed the idea on the grounds that using a cutter would amount to culpable violence, which would alienate individuals, thus deterring them from joining in the action, and provide an excuse for police repression. As an alternative to cutting the fence, thus destroying private property, it was proposed that the protesters climb over it or dig a tunnel underneath.[2] However, the members of Hard Rain argued that overly symbolic actions risked distancing the anti-nuclear movement from working-class people, who were more prepared to confront the police than many members of the coalition. The "anti-cutter" faction won the day, but they did not succeed in organizing the occupation and ultimately settled for a rally outside the enclosure. A few months later it was decided to stage another occupation and this time to bring bolt cutters. The fence was breached, but behind it stood a line of police officers, whom the activists chose not to confront.

All of this illustrates the deeply ethical mindset prevailing in anarchist networks. Faced with the almost infinite power of a nuclear facility and the repressive power of the police assigned to protect it, these militants spent many hours debating whether the use of bolt cutters to open a fence would constitute an act of violence. The defenders of other ideologies often have had fewer qualms about using devices vastly more destructive than bolt cutters. The only people ever to have given the order for atomic bombs to be dropped on cities—Hiroshima and Nagasaki—were liberals.

Actually, many anarchists consider non-violence more legitimate than the use of force, which for them is justifiable only under exceptional circumstances. Among the most influential anarchist thinkers there is no consensus on the use of violence. Mikhail Bakunin (1814–1876) and Errico Malatesta (1853–1932) are the anarchist theorists most directly identified with the notion of armed revolution; both took part in a number of insurrections throughout Europe. By contrast, William Godwin (1756–1836), the English philosopher and a forerunner of anarchism, believed in the virtues of education and that to change the world one must change mentalities. Pierre-Joseph Proudhon (1809–1865) promoted education and advocated electoral and parliamentary action; in his later years, he proposed that workers organize themselves immediately on an egalitarian and libertarian basis rather than strive to overthrow the state. Emma Goldman (1869–1940) and Peter Kropotkin (1842–1921) changed their positions several times, though both consistently pointed out that anarchist violence is a great deal less deadly than that of the state. Voltairine de Cleyre (1866–1912) noted that all ideologies find ways to justify the lethal violence of their supporters. Leo Tolstoy (1828–1910) dogmatically repudiated all forms of violence and was a powerful influence on the strategic choices of Mahatma Gandhi (1869–1948), the pre-eminent non-violent activist of the twentieth century, who, though not an anarchist, had read Kropotkin's works and had respect for anarchism.[3]

Notwithstanding the special connection that is widely believed to exist between political assassinations and anarchists, followers of *every* political ideology have been involved in such attacks. Dissenting Christians encouraged the assassination of corrupt monarchs and sometimes carried out those acts. Henri III of France was killed by Jacques Clément, a Dominican friar, on August 1, 1589. Ten years later, the Spanish Jesuit Mariana wrote in his *De rege et regis institutione* (1598), that "everyone can kill [a despot] and deprive him of life and power." In 1610, François Ravaillac, who dreamed of joining the Jesuits, stabbed Henry IV to death. Anti-monarchists, too, have assassinated heads of state. Charles I of England, in 1649, and Louis XVI of France, in 1793, were decapitated during moments of revolutionary ferment; Carlos I of Portugal was shot to death in 1908. No anarchists took part in the assassinations of Abraham Lincoln and John F. Kennedy (as far as we know), or in the failed attempts on the lives of Ronald Reagan, Charles de Gaulle, and John Paul II. Many heads of state have been assassinated in the wake of a coup d'état or a revolution, among them Patrice Lumumba in the Congo, Thomas Sanaka in Burkina Faso, and Nicolae and Elena Ceausescu in Romania. No anarchists were involved in those killings. The Red Brigades, who assassinated the Italian prime minister Aldo Moro in 1978, were Marxist-Leninists. In India, Mahatma Gandhi, Indira Gandhi, and finally her son Rajiv Gandhi were killed without the slightest involvement of anarchists. Egyptian president Anwar Sadat was murdered by "Islamist" soldiers of his own army, and Israeli prime minister Yitzhak Rabin was killed by a Jewish nationalist. Nationalists of all stripes have assassinated far more heads of state than anarchists. The presidents of Rwanda and Burundi lost their lives on April 6, 1994, when their airplane was brought down by a missile; the Rwandan prime minister was killed the following day by soldiers of the regular armed forces; these actions plunged the region into genocide. Add to this list state-sponsored terrorism and as well as the attempts, successful or not, on the lives of heads of state directly or indirectly orchestrated by, for instance, the United States: Fidel Castro, Che Guevara, Salvador Allende, Muammar Qaddafi, and others. As part of their "war on terrorism," the United States today practises targeted killings—often by drones—of the leaders of Islamist networks in Afghanistan, Pakistan, and elsewhere. And for years, the Israeli armed forces have been eliminating Palestinian leaders through targeted killings.

The official history of modern liberal states is replete with violent direct actions carried out by individuals who today are hailed as heroes for having furthered the cause of freedom, equality, and justice. On December 16, 1773, when North America was still under Britain's imperial yoke, colonists in Boston donned disguises to avoid recognition, slipped into the harbour in canoes, boarded three ships, and dumped their cargoes of tea into the water. These "vandals" destroyed several tons of merchandise to denounce the taxes imposed by Great Britain on imported goods and the Crown's financial subsidies to the East India Company. This was, in a sense, direct action in support of free trade. At the time, the British colonial authorities and moderate American patriots like George Washington saw this as little more than vandalism and illegitimate violence. Today, however, the patriots who staged the Boston Tea Party are regarded as heroes of the movement that led to the independence of the United States of America. Similarly, the French Revolution involved a multitude of direct actions, the most renowned of course being the storming of the Bastille prison in Paris by a large crowd on July 14, 1789. Bastille Day was later proclaimed the French national holiday and to this day is celebrated with great pomp by the President of the Republic and the armed forces. All of this prompted a woman who took part in the Black Bloc in Toronto in 2010 to deplore the "hypocri[sy] of bourgeois states [that] call us terrorists, while celebrating, for instance, July 4th in the United States and July 14th in France, dates that marked the culmination of bloody revolutions."[4]

Almost all of today's liberal regimes, which claim to embody values of freedom, equality, and justice, were founded through acts far more violent than the direct actions carried out by present-day activists. The United States, after winning its War of Independence, conquered the Native Americans through a series of wars. Modern France emerged as a result of several revolutions, not to mention colonialist wars. Liberalism was imposed on Germany through a military conquest, and on Japan with the help of atomic bombs. Once established, the liberal state strives to inculcate the population with the idea that it alone is entitled to employ political violence. Political authorities organize public events to underscore their claims to a monopoly on violence. The major international summits are examples of this; they serve as opportunities for these leaders to deploy thousands of heavily armed and highly visible police officers. Honour guards, shouldering arms in full dress uniform, greet foreign dignitaries as they step out of their airplanes to the sound of national anthems, many of which glorify martial values. Some examples: "perilous fight" and "bombs bursting in air" amid "battle's confusion," followed by the rallying cry "then conquer we must," in the *Star Spangled Banner*; "thy arm ready to wield the sword" in *O Canada!* (in the original French version); and, of course, the bloodthirsty refrain of *La Marseillaise*, which calls for the "impure blood" of the enemy to "water our furrows." Briefly put, claims to a monopoly on violence underpin the state's political authority. This authority, however liberal the state may be, ultimately rests on the violence of its police and armed forces.

Western governments and their supporters go so far as to back groups engaging in violent direct actions against enemy regimes. Two well-known examples, from the 1980s, were the armed militias of "freedom fighters"—the *mujahedeen* of Afghanistan and the *contras* of Nicaragua—funded and armed by the United States. The CIA produced and distributed a *Manual for Freedom Fighters* that instructed Nicaraguans opposed to the socialist Sandinista regime on how to make Molotov cocktails and use them to attack police stations.[5] Liberal politicians and journalists have often shown sympathy and respect for rioters confronting police forces in foreign states; in 1989, for example, a crowd of "youths" battered the Berlin Wall with sledgehammers.[6] Not one Western journalist or observer tried to minimize the political import of these violent acts by depicting the men and women committing them as drunken, thrill-seeking "young rioters" or "thugs."

Conservatives, too, have resorted to direct action when political authorities make decisions contrary to their interests. On the night of April 24, 1849, in Montreal, then the capital of Canada, the Parliament building was set ablaze by an angry mob that also sabotaged the city's firefighting equipment and attacked the governor's entourage. The crowd was composed almost exclusively of members of the city's Anglo elite. Over the following days, the prime minister's residence was attacked twice; the Cyrus Hotel, where the inquiry into the torching of Parliament was under way, was also set on fire. The "vandals" in this case were reacting to Parliament's decision to compensate French Canadian victims of repression in the aftermath of the republican Patriots' failed uprising of 1837–38. It is worth noting, moreover, that Montreal's Anglo elite was all the more enraged because for a number of years the British government had been threatening to drive many of its members into bankruptcy with a free trade policy that would deprive Canadian exporters of preferential tariffs in British markets.[7] More recently, in France in the early months of 2013, hundreds of thousands marched in opposition to a new law allowing same-sex marriage. The demonstrations ended in riots, with groups of homophobes and neo-fascists attacking journalists and throwing stones and bottles at the police. Finally, turning to religious mythology, one finds, once again, heroes who are perfectly ready to destroy commercial property. According to legend, Jesus drove the Jerusalem merchants from the temple with a whip and cast their money and ritual offerings on the ground. This is the act that is reputed to have convinced the Jewish religious authorities that Jesus had gone too far and deserved the death penalty.[8]

It is true that over a century ago, anarchists did assassinate several reigning monarchs and presidents. Their primary purpose was to avenge the deaths of comrades and workers at the hands of executioners, police officers, or strike breakers, by singling out the political figures deemed responsible for the bloody repression. Anarchists also expressed solidarity with far left, vaguely Marxist and libertarian terrorist groups that in the 1960s and 1970s were active in Germany (Red Army Faction), Italy (Red Brigades), and France (Action directe) and that were involved to varying degrees in the assassination of politicians, military officers, and the heads of major corporations. In every case, the terrorists' ultimate aspiration of seeing the masses rise up in a great revolutionary surge was never realized, and the ensuing repression inflicted on the protest movement as a whole was exceedingly harsh. Indeed, certain voices on the left and the far left (echoing statements made on the right and by security "experts") have warned Black Blockers against the "temptation of terrorism."[9]

Regarding terrorist organizations, activists appear to have drawn some lessons from past experience. Sofiane, who in recent years participated in political riots in Europe, declares his solidarity with the members of France's now-defunct Action directe, but adds that "we don't agree with what they did. We're sufficiently aware of global political history over the past 50 years to avoid repeating the same mistakes."[10] But on May 5, 2010, during a massive demonstration in Athens against the government's austerity policies, a group of anarchists threw a Molotov cocktail at a bank despite efforts by other anarchists to dissuade them. Three bank employees died of asphyxiation. In the wake of this event, anarchist collectives published many texts. Notwithstanding rumours that the assailants had actually been *agents provocateurs* belonging to the police, some anarchists made no effort to distance themselves from the attack, stating that Greek society was in the grip of a social war in which there was no neutral position and that bank employees were not altogether blameless. In many other texts, however, the authors sought to dissociate themselves from the lethal attack, using one of two lines of argument. The first position, representing a minority, was that anarchism had become too dogmatic and must be abandoned and replaced by post-anarchism, that is, an anarchism unfettered by dogmatic references to the historical workers' movement and the revolutionary myth. The second, endorsed by the majority of organizations associated with "official" anarchism, accepted a share of the responsibility for what had transpired, inasmuch as they viewed themselves as guardians of the anarchist tradition and regretted having let the activists who had torched the bank assume a militant posture that amounted to little more than rioting, the fetishizing of violence, and the adoption of what in effect was an anti-society attitude. A few of the texts rebuked the "anarcho-patriarchs" (i.e., veteran anarchists) for taking up too much space in the movement, thereby alienating younger militants, who then chose to play at rioting.[11] Overall, the vast majority of Greek anarchists felt that the attack on the bank had not been intended to cause death, but neither was it a model of successful or indeed desirable action.[12]

Still in Greece, some activists, such as the members of the Revolutionary Struggle organization, claimed in 2011, in a communiqué from prison, "that armed struggle is over time an integral part of the revolutionary movement of the struggle and social revolution. That armed struggle is more suitable and necessary than ever, especially under the current conditions of economic crisis." In their communiqué, Pola Roupa, Kostas Gournas, and Nikos Maziotis explained that they "come from the anarchist milieu and have many years of experience participating in mass events, demonstrations, squats; in clashes in the streets and assemblies, as well as, some of us, experience of participating in collectives and groups."[13]

Although a few proposals made by Black Bloc supporters lean toward a clandestine, rather hierarchical organization moving in the direction of armed struggle, and even a military-style mass organization,[14] activists by and large seem critical of this sort of approach (although solidarity with those facing repression and imprisonment is always necessary and important). In the words of a militant who acknowledges having confronted police and destroyed some symbols of capitalism, "armed struggle is elitist activity conducted by a small group meeting in secret. This is bullshit—we will all do it for ourselves."[15] Even those who feel, for example, that "capital is waging war against us," and that the deadly structural violence of the system is equivalent to a kind of "social war," do not stockpile weapons or pursue training in how to use them, apart from a few Molotov cocktails. Today's anarchists may talk or dream about "revolution," but they are not preparing for one.

In reality, and despite a genuine renewal, anarchism remains a relatively weak social movement, one that gave up the armed struggle long ago and whose actions are incomparably less violent than those of the state. Still, anarchist discourse—in analytical texts, pamphlets, songs, and graffiti—abounds with calls to revolt against the police, the state, and capitalism. The Anarchist Youth Network of Britain and Ireland declared in 2003: "We want to destroy government and rich people's privileges ... Capitalism must be fought in the streets."[16] That is why there is also a tendency to associate the Black Bloc with insurrectionary anarchism, which valorizes sabotage and rioting, echoing the discourse of Alfredo M. Bonanno in *Armed Joy*, or of *The Coming Insurrection* by the Comité invisible (Invisible Committee). To quote the pamphlet *Some Notes on Insurrectionary Anarchism*,

As anarchists, the revolution is our constant point of reference ...
Precisely because it is a concrete event, it must be built daily through

more modest attempts which do not have all the liberating char-
acteristics of the social revolution in the true sense. These more
modest attempts are insurrections ... The passage from the various insurrections—limited and circumscribed—to revolution can
never be guaranteed in advance by any method. What the system
is afraid of is not these acts of sabotage in themselves, so much as
their spreading socially.[17]

In a more poetic vein, following the demonstrations against the G8
in Germany in 2007, a communiqué put out by two anarchists of the
Calisse Brigade under the title "A. Anti. Anti-Capitalista!" declared,

Similar to love, a riot can sometimes take us by surprise, when we
think we are not prepared, but if we have an open disposition, a
riot, like love, will allow us to seize opportunities and situations. It
would be futile to say that we can prepare a riot, though we can at
least prepare *for* riots: do what it takes to help ignite the fire.[18]

Is Political Violence "Effective"?

Ideological and moral debates aside, history and sociology unfortunately provide no clear answer to the question of the political "effectiveness" of social movements, demonstrations, and tactics, whether
violent or non-violent. Analyses of this issue are rare and their results
inconsistent.[19] Steven E. Barkan and Lynne L. Snowden conclude that
with regard to collective actions, since we can't know for sure what the
difference is between violence and non-violence, we can't determine
the best strategies for achieving the changes that protest groups seek.[20]

The debate over violent versus non-violent tactics is all the more
inevitable because it is extremely difficult to agree on the criteria for
judging the effectiveness of a social movement or even a demonstration (as acknowledged, among others, by the anarchist activist and
writer Randall Amster).[21] What is the measure of a demonstration's success? The degree of attention received from political leaders, the general public, the media? The extent to which the political and economic

life of the city or country is disrupted? The fact, however shocking, of being arrested or even beaten by the police—something that Gandhi and his supporters invited at times—so as to expose the dark side of the "rule of law"? The increased personal prestige of the demonstration's organizers?

Furthermore, beyond any single demonstration, how can the broader objectives of a social movement be defined? If one considers, for example, the movement against capitalist globalization, is the goal to bring down capitalism or to reform it? If the latter, will the actions of the Black Blocs and their allies hinder the non-violent activists demanding reforms, or will such actions, because they are so high-profile, exert pressure on the political authorities to the point of hastening reforms? Is it a matter, finally, of exchanging one political elite for another—more specifically, of replacing the current leaders with spokespersons for major organizations in the alter-globalization movement or anti-austerity campaigns?

With regard to anarchists' collective mobilization, Randall Amster says that one might also be concerned about

the utility of disruptive tactics; cultural changes rather than only political or economic ones; the directionality of change rather than only just specific outcomes; the reclamation of space for movement activities; changing the salience of issues in the public debate; reframing the meanings of terms and interactions; focusing on the empowerment and identity constructions of movement actors; highlighting the worthiness and commitment of participants; the creation of a "credible threat" to established authorities; and the level of repression experienced by the movement, either overtly or covertly.[22]

In any case, the "effectiveness" of a militant action or a social movement must always be examined. Was it able to mobilize people? Increase media exposure? Shift the balance of power *vis-à-vis* one's enemies? Win over allies and play a leading role among them? Provide an example for the populations one claims to represent? Obtain more resources through public funding? Affect the outcome of elections? In addition, the "effectiveness" of a social movement or a demonstration must be determined in relation to the heterogeneity of the participants, who will view that effectiveness differently depending on whether they are new to the movement, veterans of autonomous activism, volunteers in a militant organization, employees of a community association, militants dreaming of a career in a political party, individuals with official titles in their organizations (e.g., president, treasurer, media spokesperson), and so forth. Academics and militant "leaders," however, tend to conceive of effectiveness in terms of systemic gains, that is, stronger representation in official institutions and a greater share of collective resources.[23] The tendency to reduce a movement's effectiveness to its potential for bringing its "representatives" into the decision-making process of the institutions overseeing economic globalization is precisely why organization leaders are inclined to condemn the Black Blocs (a point examined below).

This dynamic is not unique to the alter-globalization movement. Frances Piven and Richard Cloward, as well as other sociologists, have described how the self-proclaimed leaders of a social movement are likely to keep its members disciplined so that the official political elite will acknowledge the "leaders" as the only responsible and respectable representatives of the movement.[24] Yet ironically, the direct actions of the Black Blocs and their allies may have positive effects for the reformists who are so ready to censure them. For the actions—indeed, the very existence—of the Black Blocs and their allies have the potential to send shock waves through the entire political sphere, obliging officials and reformist office-holders to reposition themselves, and engendering debates, struggles, and shifts in alliances, strategies, and orientations that can transform the economic and political status quo, give rise to negotiations, and ultimately generate reforms. Reforms brought about by radical actions—a paradox? Not really. Indeed, the use of force by certain components of a broad social movement can benefit the very people who condemn this tactical choice.

The classic examples of Mahatma Gandhi and Martin Luther King are enlightening in this regard. Official history ascribes great political and moral wisdom to these two celebrated advocates of non-violent direct action. They are often described as having triumphed solely through non-violent practices. Yet each was part of a vast movement encompassing political actors who did resort to force and who carried out armed assaults against the police and the military. Would non-violent activists have succeeded on their own, without the violence of their allies, in driving the British colonizers from India or checking racial segregation in the United States?[25] Examples from the feminist and labour movements are equally illuminating. As discussed earlier, feminists of the early 20th century, despite their marked penchant for non-violent action, sometimes resorted to force, setting fire to mail-boxes and churches, breaking store windows, occupying polling sta-tions, and destroying election ballot boxes and ballots. Around the same time, union militants, in the face of often bloody police and mil-itary repression, engaged in violent actions that punctuated the labour movement's campaigns for political rights and decent working condi-tions. As Emmeline Pankhurst recalled about the 1880s, the very early days of the suffragist movement,

> not one woman took counsel with herself as to how and why the
> agricultural labourers had won their franchise. They had won it, as
> a matter of fact, by burning hayricks, rioting, and otherwise dem-
> onstrating their strength in the only way that English politicians can
> understand. The threat to march a hundred thousand men to the
> House of Commons unless the bill was passed played its part also
> in securing the agricultural labourer his political freedom. But no
> woman suffragist noticed that.[26]

It is quite plausible that in all these cases the pressure generated by violent actions prompted the political authorities to seriously consider accepting a certain degree of emancipation with a view to isolating and neutralizing more easily those involved in such actions. In this way, the use of force may have contributed to India's independence, the end of racial segregation in the United States, and the relative emancipation of women and workers in the West. Seen in that light, the use of force in the political arena may well be an effective way to engender debate and change in situations that at first glance seem immutable.

Be that as it may, since the beginning of the alter-globalization movement it has not been at all clear what effect, if any, *peaceful* mobilizations and protests have had on neoliberalism and capitalism. Ward Churchill, in his study *Pacifism as Pathology*, warns against dogmatic advocates of non-violence, who willingly labour under the "pathological" illusion that a candlelight vigil in front of, for example, the headquarters of the war department, is an "effective" way to stop a war (just as it would be absurd to suppose that hurling a stone at a bank window disrupts capitalism; in both cases the action is ultimately a symbolic one, expressive to varying degrees of a more or less potent critique). The anarchist activist Tammy Kovich, who marched with the Black Bloc at the Toronto G20 Summit, has stated,

> The pacifist position is accepted without question, while advocates of more aggressive tactics are put on the defensive. We need to turn the debate on its head—given the severity of the situation we face, in light of the pervasive nature of the systems of domination and oppression that we oppose, and acknowledging the pressing need for an intensification of our struggle, we need to begin asking ourselves if *non-violence* can be justified.[27]

In the current non-revolutionary context, radicals, instead of biding their time while they watch for the advent of a new world, fight in the existing world to open up and enlarge spaces of freedom, equality, and justice. Activists may find this frustrating inasmuch as it bespeaks their lack of control over the potentially reformist repercussions of their political actions. But so it goes for any political actor in a complex world.[28]

Outside the debates in the alternative media, however, the message of this political "violence" remains generally misunderstood. Considering how they are vilified by the mainstream media, which, at the same time, massively promote consumerism, the Black Blocs and their allies will have to carry out many more direct actions for material goods to lose their sacred status and for Black Blockers to make a difference on the political scene.

Yet the Black Blocs have garnered some sympathetic responses. Indeed, their actions have sometimes been praised by those non-violent protesters who realize that force is sometimes necessary to boost the visibility and dynamism of progressive campaigns. Black Blocs are often accompanied by dozens or even hundreds of demonstrators whose presence testifies to their symbolic, moral, and political support. This was the case, for instance, when radical feminist blocs waved black and purple flags (the anarchist-feminist colours) at the Toronto G20 Summit in 2010 and during the May Day demonstration in Montreal in 2012. A journalist covering the No TAV protests in Italy in 2011 quoted "an elderly lady" on the subject of the Black Blocs: "They may be anarchist, but we should thank them anyway because they are doing something for us."[29]

The Target Is the Message

Protest is never organized haphazardly; its targets are always chosen for their symbolic value. Clément Barette interviewed participants in political riots in Europe and reported that "all the subjects asserted that targets were chosen because of the symbolic weight attributed to them. Almost all stressed that certain ethical principles were applied to the destruction [of the targets], with respect to the projected image of the riot as well as personal, political, and social 'morals.'"[30]

On the subject of the Black Bloc presence at the Occupy Oakland rally, an anonymous commentator observed:

> To the pleasure of a great majority of the several hundred demonstrators, an active minority within the march set about attacking a series of targets: Chase Bank, Bank of America, Wells Fargo, Whole Foods, the UC Office of the President ... The choice of these targets seems intuitive to anyone attuned to the political climate of Oakland. The banks attacked are responsible for tens of thousands of foreclosures in Oakland alone ... Despite any number [of] reasons to destroy these places, the remarkable point of these attacks

was that no justification was necessary. As each pane of glass fell to the floor and each ATM was put out of service, cheers would consistently erupt. In 1999, at the height of neoliberal prosperity, participants in the black bloc at the Seattle WTO summit issued a communiqué detailing the crimes of their targets. A dozen years and a worldwide crisis later, such an indictment would seem silly. Everyone hates these places."[31]

On principle, Black Blocs do not strike community centres, public libraries, the offices of women's committees, or even small independent businesses; their attacks focus on the soulless premises of large corporations. Again, the target is the message. Critics of the Black Blocs have often pointed out that amid all the confusion, small independent businesses have been attacked. In his article "The Cancer of Occupy," Chris Hedges asserts that "groups of Black Bloc protesters, for example, smashed the windows of a locally owned coffee shop in November in Oakland and looted it."[32] Admittedly, the targets of Black Bloc actions are not always emblematic of the state or of corporate capitalism. On May Day 2013, in Seattle, the police broke up a demonstration and some protesters reacted by smashing windows, including those of a local bar named Bill's Off Broadway. According to an observer, activists were saying: "I'd gladly smash a Bank of America window, but I'd never—and I don't know anyone who would ever—want to break the window of a neighbourhood bar or pizzeria. What the hell happened there?"

Then who did it? Was it random free agents with no political consciousness, or was it "demonstrators who forgot the 'targeted' part of 'targeted property damage'"? In any case, a group named the Anarchists of Puget Sound sent this message: "We support everything that happened last night but feel that it is our responsibility to support our neighborhood small businesses as well ... We would like to throw a benefit for Bill's Off Broadway and other small businesses to help them with the cost of replacing their windows."[33]

My own observations are that it is quite exceptional for Black Blockers to smash the windows of small shops. In any case, it is prudent to investigate further before concluding that merely gratuitous

For three days in April 2009, thousands of protesters in Strasbourg, some peaceful, some militant, marked the 60th anniversary of NATO.

violence was involved. In Montreal, for example, the glass door of a pizzeria was broken during a demonstration; what came to light a few days later was that several police officers had taken shelter in the restaurant after apprehending a protester and that the Black Bloc had been attempting to free their comrade. In Strasbourg in April 2009, a Black Bloc threw a Molotov cocktail at an Ibis Hotel. Why?, I asked myself, notwithstanding that Ibis is a major international hotel. Several years later, from a pamphlet about that specific mobilization, I learned why the activists had considered it a legitimate target: the hotel had housed journalists attending the official NATO meeting; police were hiding in it to spy on protesters, and it was regularly making a profit from refugees who were in the process of being expelled.[34] Concerning the incident in Oakland, the graphic journalist Susie Cagle explained: "The 'local coffee shop' vandalism Hedges contends was committed by

Black Bloc [activists] was in fact one window of a corporate coffee chain smashed ... and by someone not wearing a mask, not wearing black."[35]

Over the years, more and more witnesses have come forward to recount that Black Blocs have often protected other demonstrators against police assaults. During the debate in the United States about the presence of Black Blocs in Occupy Movement demonstrations, a journalist-activist declared: "I have seen black blocs de-arresting their comrades [stealing people back from police custody], without hurting anyone or anything ... I have seen them returning tear gas canisters from whence they came in order to mitigate the suffering of children and elderly protesters in their midst."[36]

During the Quebec student strike of 2012, a number of statements on the Web thanked the Black Blocs for protecting or rescuing demonstrators from police brutality. A 67-year-old man posted this comment on the blog of Jean-François Lisée, a well-known Quebec journalist and politician:

> Yesterday my wife and I went to join the young people in the streets. A police officer called my wife an old bag so I went over to give him a piece of my mind and he pepper-sprayed me. A Black Bloc member came to help me and splashed a liquid on my eyes that eased the pain. Before, I was afraid of the young masked Black Blockers ... Not any more. Now I'm afraid of the young masked officers of the SPVM (Montreal police force).[37]

Similarly, after seeing the Black Bloc lob tear gas canisters back at the police, erect barricades, and provide first aid to the injured, a female protester wrote on Facebook:

> I didn't hear anyone thank the members of the Black Bloc and the other radicals who had the courage to put themselves between the police and the population ... THANK YOU ... I refuse to condemn you ... I hope you won't have to intervene again. I would like for your presence to be unnecessary ... But you are actually the last defensive wall for people trying to exercise their democratic rights.[38]

A Black Blocker kicks a tear gas canister back at police during the Quebec Liberal Party Congress of May 4, 2012, Victoriaville, Quebec.

Heart Attack protest against the 2010 Olympics, Granville Street, Vancouver, Canada, February 13, 2010.

Anarchist Violence and Respect for Tactical Diversity

The violence versus non-violence debate is a perennial source of tension in progressive and radical circles, where the ethics of using force are of greater concern than they apparently are for the political elites, including liberals. In the early 1990s, the expression "fluffy vs spiky" was how English-speaking activists characterized the debate.[39] In those oversimplified terms, the Black Blocs are of course quintessentially "spiky." In reality, however, such distinctions are moot. In 2000, during the anti-IMF/World Bank rally in Prague, the Black Bloc brought a beach ball four metres across to play with the water cannon, but it also threw Molotov cocktails at the police.[40] At the same event, a member of the Tactical Frivolity collective, composed of women disguised as giant fairies and associated with the Pink & Silver Bloc, expressed her weariness with the "fluffy vs spiky" debate. One might have expected her to categorically condemn all violence. Instead she wondered: "What is violence anyway when the State is, like, killing people every day, man. And the people in the World Bank eat Third World babies for breakfast, so if they get bricked then, hey, that's their fault."[41]

Yet it is not unusual for debates, shouting matches, and even scuffles to break out among protesters, with "violent" activists being laid into by "non-violent" activists or the "peace police"—as they were dubbed in "A Communiqué from one section of the Black Bloc of N30 in Seattle," sent out on the Web after the demonstrations in 1999. To quote from that communiqué: "On at least six separate occasions, so-called 'non-violent' activists physically attacked individuals who targeted corporate property. Some even went so far as to stand in front of the Niketown super store and tackle and shove the black bloc away."[42] More than ten years later, during the Occupy rally in Oakland, Black Blockers were jostled by "non-violent" demonstrators, one of whom threatened them with martial arts moves. More recently, during the Quebec student strike of 2012, "non-violent" protesters assaulted members of the Black Bloc, manhandling them or tackling them from behind and pinning them to the ground. Two demonstrators were even proud to tell the media, with reference to broken windows: "We don't want that. Okay, so in the streets tonight we're taking the law into our own hands!"[43]

Those "peace police" activists were clearly authoritarian and repressive in their efforts to impose non-violence by force. But does this mean that a group of a few dozen amilitants can legitimately use force against symbols of capitalism or the police during a demonstration at the risk of turning the thousands of other protesters into targets of police violence?

For a few of the mobilizations that took place around 2000, it was proposed to identify certain areas of the city by colours so as to allow different types of demonstrations to be held simultaneously. This was done at the Reclaim the Street rally in London on June 18, 1999; at the first Global Day of Action called by Peoples' Global Action (PGA), an anti-capitalist network founded in Geneva in 1998 and close to the Zapatista rebels; at the protest marches against the IMF and World Bank in Washington in April 2000; and in Prague on September 26, 2000, for the protest against the IMF and World Bank Summit. Colour coding made it possible to distinguish among three separate marches: blue for the Black Bloc, accompanied by the Infernal Noise Brigade marching band; yellow for the Tute Bianche; pink for the Pink and Silver Bloc.[44] In Prague, it was necessary to establish a "separation between permitted and non-permitted events by time and space to insure safe space for internationals, high risk folks or others who want to be assured of avoiding police repression in any form." It was also important to cultivate a "sense of unity between all aspects of the action whether permitted or non-permitted."[45] In Montreal, militants belonging to the Convergence des luttes anticapitalistes (CLAC: Convergence of Anti-Capitalist Struggles) believed that in order to facilitate tactical diversity, appropriate forms of mobilization, organization, and discourse would be needed.

In 2001, CLAC, together with the Comité d'accueil du Sommet des Amériques (CASA: Welcome Committee for the Summit of the Americas), proposed a new concept, "respect for diversity of tactics," a principle that valorized political autonomy while also stressing the legitimacy of multiple forms of protest within a single movement.[46] The expression was not altogether new. For instance, it had been used in the United States in 1990 during discussions on the antiwar movement as a whole, which, it was argued, should accept legal, peaceful demonstrations as well as acts of sabotage.[47]

CLAC, founded in April 2000, specialized in organizing demonstrations—putting up mobilization posters, renting trucks and music equipment, distributing food and water, setting up teams to provide medical and legal assistance, and so on. But it did not participate directly in the actions of affinity groups and individual protesters. Respect for diversity of tactics and the deliberate absence of marshals meant that those taking part in CLAC rallies could carry out actions within a very broad spectrum ranging from street theatre to attacks on symbolic targets. This meant that CLAC's "media committees" would not denounce the actions of the Black Blocs and their allies in their public statements. Furthermore, when organizing a demonstration, CLAC identified three zones: "green," "yellow," and "red." The green zone was a sanctuary where demonstrators were, theoretically, in no danger of being arrested. The yellow zone was for those undertaking nonviolent civil disobedience and involved a minor risk of being arrested. The red zone was for protesters who were ready for more aggressive tactics, including skirmishing with the police. These spatial divisions were also meant to allow protesters who were unwilling to take part in such confrontations or risk being arrested to openly associate with radical organizations like CLAC. Note, however, that the police in Montreal and Quebec City have not always abided by these divisions. Indeed, they have attacked "green" zones on a number of occasions; for example, they arrested 240 people assembled in a green zone during rallies against the WTO in Montreal in July 2003.

CLAC was able to articulate the concept of "respect for diversity of tactics" thanks not only to the valorization of the autonomy of collective action among its members but also to international circumstances and the particular context of activism in Montreal at the time. In the late 1990s many CLAC members had worked in SalAMI, a group established to protest against the Multilateral Agreement on Investment (MAI, or AMI in French) through non-violent civil disobedience and voluntary mass arrests. Over time, SalAMI grew increasingly authoritarian, its leaders more and more inclined to "moralize" about non-violence. On several occasions they even publicly admonished the "vandals" belonging to other militant groups.[48] At a rally held in Montreal on March 15, 2000, by the Collectif opposé à la brutalité policière (COBP: Committee Opposed to Police Brutality), demonstrators clashed with the police, a McDonald's and some banks were attacked, and over 100 people were arrested. SalAMI's leaders, along with those of the Mouvement action justice (MAJ: Justice Action Movement), publically condemned the "vandals." At that point a number of militants abandoned SalAMI and joined CLAC or other militant groups promoting respect for tactical diversity.

Finally, CLAC's declared position in favour of tactical diversity was intended to foster greater awareness among Western activists of the significance of "violence." As a member of Peoples' Global Action (PGA), CLAC thought it useful to recall that what in the West is perceived as "violent"—taking down a fence, breaking a window, throwing a stone at a police officer—may seem trivial from the standpoint of the protest and resistance movements of the "South," where political and economic conflicts are far more polarized, protesters often risk their lives when taking action, and the use of weapons such as machetes or even firearms is at times considered necessary to prevent massacres at the hands of police, military, or paramilitary forces.[49] CLAC embraced PGA principles proposing, among other things, the adoption of a "confrontational attitude, since we do not think that lobbying can have a major impact in such biased and undemocratic organisations," and the employment of "direct action and civil disobedience."[50]

Respect for tactical diversity is also consistent with anarchism. Indeed, what sets anarchism plainly apart from other political ideologies is not its attitude toward violence, but its profound respect for equality and individual freedom. Clément Barette has interviewed a number of French citizens who have taken part in demonstrations. He notes that they define themselves as "anarchists," "autonomous activists (*autonomes*)," "communists," and "libertarian communists." He adds that, beyond the welter of labels, "autonomy in decision-making and action [is] the main criterion ... with regard to political activity or the recourse to violence."[51]

However, among Black Blockers and their allies there are some who occasionally adopt a dogmatic and disdainful stance toward those who do not use force, an attitude expressed in their refusal to debate in good faith at meetings where preparations for a demonstration are being discussed. At such times, the notion of respect for tactical diversity may be used disingenuously as an excuse for not considering the viewpoints of those who are uncomfortable with rowdy demonstrations.[52] On the whole, however, Black Blockers have no problem respecting tactical diversity and the plurality of collective actions at demonstrations: marching peacefully with signs, flags, and slogans; staging sit-ins or die-ins and non-violent blocking actions; performing street theatre, music, and giant puppet shows; displaying large banners and writing graffiti; and, possibly, resorting to force. Indeed, Black Bloc activists are well aware that many anarchists and anarchist sympathizers, including close friends and relations, engage in non-violent civil disobedience and peaceful demonstrations, and that their choices must be respected and their safety ensured.[53] An interviewee who participated in various affinity groups within Black Blocs said: "I never obliged anyone to throw anything. I'm for the diversity of tactics and there are Black Bloc members who don't want to use force and who form affinity groups of volunteers, medics, for example."[54] A Boston resident who had participated in various demonstrations without ever having used force said in an interview that "*respect for the diversity of tactics* is essential. Each person must do what she or he thinks is right ... When it comes to violence ... I know perfectly well that I don't have all the answers on the subject of violence/non-violence, so I'm not going to prevent people from doing what they want to do; I don't want that sort of power."[55]

Tactical diversity sometimes takes the form of parallel demonstrations, such as those organized recently for May Day in Berlin and Montreal. In the march held by labour unions, demonstrators were kept in line by a corps of marshals, while a separate anti-capitalist march was more tolerant of direct actions. During the protests against the Toronto G20 Summit in 2010, the Black Bloc and its allies split off from the mass demonstration, dashing in the opposite direction to attack symbols of capitalism. Throughout the Quebec student strike of 2012 there were calls for autonomous "disruptive actions."

In other situations, after some windows were broken at large demonstrations, a number of people angrily accused the Black Blocs of endangering protesters who had decided to march peacefully. Notwithstanding their abundant references to equality and citizens' participation, very few progressive organizations respect tactical diversity and applaud pluralism among activists. In fact, most spokespersons for reformist groups find such an approach intolerable. Surprisingly, the same has been true of the Convergence des luttes antiautoritaire et anticapitaliste (CLAAACG8: Convergence of Anti-Authoritarian and Anti-Capitalist Struggles), an umbrella organization of French and European anarchists, including Alternative libertaire, the Confédération nationale du travail, Fédération anarchiste, Organisation communiste libertaire, Organisation socialiste libertaire, and the Réseau No Pasaran. CLAAACG8 was founded during the run-up to the June 2003 G8 Summit in Évian. Its aim was to enable those all too often rival groups to unite their forces and co-operate with social democratic organizations in the massive unitary march protesting the Summit. One of its goals was institutional in nature—that is, to see its red and black contingent surpass in number those of other participating organizations, such as the LCR, the Greens, and ATTAC, which had jointly negotiated the route and the march's security arrangements with the French and Swiss authorities. Mission accomplished (if one credits the reports in *Le Monde*), to the great delight of the anarchist organizers.[56]

But this political choice had meant reining in the protesters to keep things from getting out of hand (thereby ensuring the success of the organizers' institutional strategy and projecting the desired public image of the CLAAACG8). While paying lip service to tactical diversity, CLAAACG8 had put together its own corps of marshals and had made it known that the red and black contingent would not allow itself to serve as the "aircraft carrier" (as one organizer put it) for those planning militant direct actions. The reason given for all this was that demonstrators unwilling to confront the police should not be put in harm's way.[57] As it turned out, the CLAAACG8 contingent did take part in the very peaceful "unitary" march, but by then, a series of disruptive actions had already taken place, earlier that morning, far from the site of the mass demonstration.

CLAAACG8's "institutional" approach was deplored by a number of autonomous groups and individuals, who were deeply disappointed to see anarchist groups surfing the alter-globalization wave and measuring the success of their own mobilizations by comparing them to those of the social democrats and in terms of the mainstream media coverage. In response, a handful of anarchists from Strasbourg and elsewhere formed a contingent that identified itself as the "CLAAAC réfractaire" (Insubordinate CLAAAC), which marched directly behind the marshals of the official CLAAACG8 chanting slogans about the "libertarian police." The Humus Bloc, for its part, put out a sarcastic statement concerning the "security arrangements of the demonstration made in agreement with the police to prevent 'vandals' from executing any 'terrorist' actions," and asking if it was "necessary to negotiate the self-management (*autogestion*) of demonstrations with the cops."[58]

Performative Symbolism

The Pink Bloc carnivalesque protest actions like the one just described can be problematic for elites precisely *because* they are carried out in a largely festive spirit. Similarly, the Black Blocs "play" at incarnating the character of the "violent anarchist," at once adopting and shaping the image associated with anarchists in the Western imagination. According to the anarchist activist and anthropologist David Graeber, even the most aggressive actions taken by Black Blocs have more to do with spectacle than with actual violence.

Many elements of the popular rebellions in medieval Western societies have endured and re-emerged in the large anti-capitalist rallies of the late 20th and early 21st centuries. In the Middle Ages,[59] the people often took advantage of carnival days, when the streets belonged to them, to express—sometimes festively, sometimes violently—their dissatisfaction with the political, religious, or economic authorities. Anonymity was a concern even then, and scholars of popular protest movements have identified a "tradition of anonymity"—a tradition worth upholding today, given that as the powers-that-be have no misgivings about meting out punishment to those who defy them.[60] Behind their disguises and masks, the people who joined in the medieval celebrations felt less exposed to the brutality of the authorities. Centuries later, during the 2001 Summit of the Americas in Quebec City, members of the Black Bloc wore masks on which the following statement was printed in English and French: "We will remain faceless because we refuse the spectacle of celebrity, because we are everyone, because the carnival beckons, because the world is upside down, because we are everywhere. By wearing masks we show that who we are is not as important as what we want, and what we want is everything for everyone."[61] Medieval carnivals also made it less hazardous to express anger, whether through laughter and satire, symbolic violence (e.g., burning effigies), or physical violence (e.g., pillaging shops known to overcharge for basic necessities, or ransacking the tax collector's residence).

International summits themselves are in fact festivals—admittedly more ceremonial than festive—where the elites occupy centre stage and put on a show for the whole world. A G20 Summit attracts thousands of journalists, who are greeted and accommodated in keeping with the detailed plans of the Summit organizers. The purpose of such events has much more to do with symbolism than decision making; most of the negotiations have already been conducted, and the major decisions have been made beforehand, at far less visible ministerial meetings. In the face of the official spectacle designed to legitimize and glorify power, the "street party" counter-spectacle strives to demonstrate the power of protest and to chip away at the aura of legitimacy of official power. It is in this light that one can interpret, for instance, the idea of the Deconstructionist Institute for Surreal Topology (DIST), a group that brought a full-size catapult to the 2001 Summit of the Americas in Quebec City. For the first time in recent history, the authorities had established a security perimeter several kilometres across, which the local population soon dubbed the "wall of shame."[62] The catapult, whose ammunition consisted exclusively of teddy bears, served to highlight the image of power entrenched behind a wall. What ensued was nothing short of a farce. Jaggi Singh, a well-known member of CLAC, was identified by the police as the leader of the Black Blocs, arrested, and detained for weeks on charges including possessing a weapon, to wit, the catapult seized by the police. This was a first in North American jurisprudence. Jaggi Singh would eventually be acquitted of all charges. Serge Ménard, Quebec's Minister of Public Security during the Summit of the Americas, formulated his personal theory about the catapult: "I know that in the long run this is part of a plan. Because at the next demonstration they organize, wherever in the world it may be, something will be hidden inside the teddy bear. It may be acid, a Molotov cocktail, bricks."[63] Twelve years after the Summit of the Americas, no other catapult has ever popped up in an alter-globalization mass demonstration.

Some activists, such as the anarchists who issued the "Manifeste du Carré Noir" (Black Square Manifesto) during the Quebec student strike of 2012, regard their attacks against public or private property not as violence but as a "political and symbolic gesture."[64] The targeting of symbols can be understood as a form of "propaganda of the deed." Destroying or pillaging merchandise enables one to openly express a radical critique of specific companies or of capitalism and consumer society in general; at the same time, it allows one to dent the sacrosanct aura surrounding consumer goods in our society.[65] A Québécois woman who had been in several Black Blocs put it this way: "Breaking a window or attacking a media vehicle is an attempt to show that material goods are not all that important."[66] Indeed, a number of those who participate in direct actions are surprised that so many people are outraged by a few broken windows, given that "property feels no pain," to borrow a phrase from graffiti written in Seattle during the events of November 30, 1999.

In his research, the anthropologist and activist Jeffrey Juris focuses on the "symbolic-expressive" aspects of what he calls "performative violence." (Another scholar, Maxime Boidy, is studying the social meaning of the Black Bloc's visual performance.) Having closely studied the Black Blocs in action at the 2001 G8 Summit in Genoa, he observes that, beyond the low-intensity "violence," the action's purpose is to "produc[e] concrete messages challenging global capitalism and the state" and "generate radical identities."[67] Graeber contends that the low intensity of the violence is exactly what perturbs the elites, because "governments simply do not know how to deal with an overtly revolutionary movement that refuses to fall into familiar patterns of armed resistance."[68] Indeed, who looks more violent? A heavily armed police officer, or an anarchist sporting a simple wool cap and a flimsy scarf for a mask? And of the two, who actually *is* more violent, at least potentially? Here is one activist's bemused response: "But come on—a stone against a helicopter, a stick against an armoured car—and they call us violent? Frankly, there is no comparison—they are the real butchers, they are the ones whose hands are soaked in blood."[69]

The Canadian artist Marc James Léger, arguing for an aesthetic approach to the issue, compares the Black Bloc's actions at the 2010 Toronto G20 Summit to a work of art, and concludes that

> such actions are not premised on their immediate fulfillment but in the communication that the desire to smash capitalism can never be satisfied with such limited gestures. The desire is deeper and spreads from one symbol to another, reproducing itself *toward* infinity. Still, as the broken window affirms, the transgression of the symbolic Law also brings on anxiety ... What movement activists should do is look indirectly at the smashed window, aesthetically perhaps.[70]

Yet some on the far left reprove the Black Blocs precisely for being content to strike the aesthetic pose of the rebel while their actions fail to significantly hinder capitalism.[71] For the Canadian anarchist Tammy Kovich, this criticism

> completely skirts the prefigurative characteristics of the bloc. It is absolutely true that smashing a window does not begin to

approximate the acts required to create a new society; however, there is more to a black bloc than the smashing of windows. The bloc, as a pulsing body on the street, is organized horizontally. Decisions are made on the ground by all participants … The picture of the bloc from the outside is very different from the reality and experience on the inside; the ethos of the black bloc is one of solidarity and collective care … Crucial to the project of creating a new society is creating new ways of being, interacting and organizing with each other.[72]

CHAPTER 3

THE ROOTS OF RAGE AGAINST THE SYSTEM

More than anything else, it is the Black Blocs' relationship with force, with "violence," that informs discussions about them. Outsiders view the Black Blocs as expressions of blind rage. Demonstrating, carrying out direct actions, and rioting all bring into question their *raison d'être*. But instead of perceiving this as a competing rationality that defines justice, freedom, equality, and security according to criteria different from their own, states and those who support them are likely to claim that nothing but irrational emotion is at work in such acts.[1] One can, of course, find anarchist ideology unattractive and have a preference for liberalism, or prefer non-violence to violence in whatever form. One can also disagree with the analyses and political motivations of the participants in Black Blocs as articulated and disseminated on anarchist websites, in fanzines and journals, or encapsulated in graffiti such as "Capitalism cannot be reformed," "No justice, no peace! Fuck the police,"[2] "Peace, love, and petrol bombs," "You make plans, we make history," "Smash false dreamland," "Squat the world,"[3] "ACAB [All Cops Are Bastards]." But disagreement cannot serve as an excuse for refusing to examine seriously the ideas and logic of those taking part in Black Blocs. To say they are merely apolitical and irrational young people is at best intellectual laziness, at worst a political lie.

Emotion

The Black Blocs can be denigrated through the suggestion that they represent nothing but pure emotion, an aggressive urge. When some shop windows were targeted in 2003 during a WTO meeting in Montreal, *La Presse* editorialist Mario Roy wrote: "Vandalism is the opposite of thought. The only thing at work here is a sensation: *pleasure.*"[4] It is true that, just as many people experience strong emotions and elation during peaceful political actions and gatherings, some derive real joy from the political use of force. To quote a European protester: "The strongest sensations I have felt came amid riots."[5] Moreover, according to an affinity group that was part of the Black Bloc in Genoa in July 2001, the monotony of today's world is why "destroying it ought to be *fun.*"[6] But this emotional impulse does not mean that such actions lack economic or political rationality.

During the mobilizations against the G8 in Germany in 2007, a network of affinity groups calling itself the "International Brigades" proposed a "Plan B" that involved demonstrating in Berlin rather than Rostock, near the site of the Summit. Though this alternative project was not a great success, the rallying call included explicit references to the joy recently experienced at the demonstration in Rostock: "Join the battle of joy … Under every mask was a smile, in every stone thrown against the common enemy there was joy, in every body revolting against oppression there was desire … Individually we are nothing, together we are power. Together we are a commune: the commune of Rostock."[7]

Joy is not the only emotion animating the Black Blocs; there is also rage. The anthropologist Sian Sullivan, an observer-participant at demonstrations against the European Union in Thessaloniki in June 2003, ties the use of force and the destruction of property by the Black Blocs and their allies to rage against an iniquitous and exploitative system that subjects most of the population to structural violence.[8] According to Sullivan, the use of force in anti-capitalist protests effectively neutralizes three basic but ultimately dead-end responses to the current political and economic system. First, social apathy, pathological passivity, and voluntary isolation.[9] Next, the recourse to individual or group psychological therapy and to spiritual development programs. Finally, the *a priori* conclusion that non-violence is rational and effective, while militant force is irrational and ineffective.[10]

Besides citing studies showing that activism boosts a person's sense of well-being and lessens the effects of depression, Sullivan suggests that activists should demand "the right to be angry."[11] In this regard, in interviews with anarchists, when I asked them if they had ever wept for political reasons, 23 out of 25 answered yes, revealing a strong emotional engagement with politics.[12] Several interviewees told me they had shed tears of rage in the face of injustice (poverty, racism, police brutality, etc.). Some activists, then, perceive militant action and indeed militant force as a legitimate way to express anger at an infuriating system. One Black Blocker said that the "Black Bloc is about taking anger and directing it toward an enemy, a rational target."[13] Similarly, an activist who had taken part in protests in Lausanne against the G8 Summit in Évian in 2003 said that "capitalism kills … It is right to respond to overwhelming injustice with anger."[14] "Anger is a gift," declared a slogan scribbled on a wall at Aristotle University in Thessaloniki during the EU Summit in June 2003.[15] Finally, in comparing their previous militant experiences in Canada with their participation in a Black Bloc in Germany in 2007, two "companer@s" of the Calisse Brigade asked with regard to the relative moderation of North American activism, "What will it take to get angry and fight?"[16]

Reason and emotion are not mutually exclusive; both can generate a political will that justifies political action. Political action—violent or not—is generated by a political will, which is itself the product of a rationale or an emotion or a blend of emotion and rationale. The few sociologists and political scientists who have investigated the role of emotions in politics have observed that both emotion and reason construct political thought and will.[17] George Katsiaficas uses the term "emotional rationality."[18] The political scientist George E. Marcus contends that citizens can be responsible and reasonable political actors only if they are emotionally engaged with respect to a given issue. Without an emotional investment in politics, why give it any thought? Why get involved?[19] In the late 19th century, Voltairine de Cleyre offered this explanation for why she was an anarchist: "Mental activity alone, however, would not be sufficient ... The second reason, therefore, why I am an Anarchist, is because of the possession of a very large proportion of sentiment ... Now my feelings have ever revolted against repression in all forms."[20]

Emotions also come into play in the formation of a rebel community and in the sharing of both the joy of finally taking action and the fear of repression. One person who took part in the "anti-cuts" protests in London in 2011 attested to this:

> It can feel exhilarating running down a street and moving as a group. It is an atmosphere of resistance, not of chaos. You could get hurt or arrested so you have a combination of fear and adrenaline and a sense that this is the moment to act because it could all end shortly. There's an intensity to the moment. It is not just about breaking things. It is manifesting your politics and personal feeling in the street.[21]

Many Black Blockers regard the joy felt or the frustration vented in the heat of action as illegitimate emotions that, like an unmentionable disease, are best kept to oneself. Others, by contrast, openly own these feelings and explain them in political and social terms. Clément Barrette notes, for example, that "the *frustration* that a number of our study's subjects spoke of seems to be a *conscious* feeling virtually owned and integrated in the process of politicization. As such, it is perceived as a driving force of collective action."[22] The emotions felt by these anarchists and their allies acquire meaning in very specific political, economic, and social circumstances, which in turn structure their political perceptions, conceptions, analyses, and arguments and affect their tactical and strategic choices. The feeling of frustration stems, in particular, from experiencing an economic and political system deemed unjust, violent, and lethal.

The notion of a restorative violence that brings joy or enables the release of frustration is consistent with the political, cultural, and artistic references shared by individuals who have engaged in direct actions. In France and Quebec, for instance, anarchists watch films like Mathieu Kassovitz's *La Haine* (1995) (a favourite among radical networks in Italy as well) and Jean-François Richet's *Ma 6-T va craquer* (1996). Both are about riots in the suburbs of France. They also listen to Bérurier Noir, a French anarcho-punk band of the 1980s, whose songs contain lyrics such as these, from "Baston," from their 1983 album, *Macadam Massacre* (our translation):

> The cops arrest us for nothing …
> They shouldn't be surprised
> To get their heads bashed.
> When they pound us it's natural
> For us to feel hatred.[23]

In English, one might listen to "One Dead Cop" by Leftover Crack: "The police kill and then they lie some more / In a conspiracy to cage the poor," and "The cops are like another gang, / only like, maybe the biggest, y'know? / We're all fuckin' helpless. / Fuck the police."

The Montreal punk band Jeunesse Apatride even titled its 2002 album *Black Bloc-n-Roll*. "Black Bloc Revenge" is the title of a song performed by the French group Brigada Flores Magon. In English, Black Blockers and rioters might listen to the songs "Sleep Now in the Fire" by Rage Against the Machine, or "Resisting Tyrannical Government" by Propagandhi, among many others. In Germany, the *Autonomen* listen to songs expressing strong anti-nationalism and referring to anti-fascist actions, such as "I Can't Love This Country" by Across the Border, "Raven gegen Deutschland" (Raver Against Germany) by Egotronic, and "Halt dein Mund" ("Shut Up") by Johnny Mauser. The song "Nazi Scums" by Skarpretter is specifically about fighting the neo-Nazis in the streets: "The antifascist black flag of anarchy / Is not for their filthy hands / NO PASARAN! / We've got an enemy to beat / We've got to meet them in the street / There's a time to fight and that time has come / Were coming for you, naziscum!"

Of course, there is no simple cause-and-effect relationship between artistic taste and direct action, such that if I listen to Bérurier Noir I

"On August 18, 1990, let's stop the Nazis from marching in Wunsiedel." Poster for an anti-fascist action to prevent a Nazi march in Wunsiedel, August 18, 1990. Wunsiedel, the site of the grave of notorious Nazi war criminal Rudolf Hess, was a place of pilgrimage for Nazis until 2005, when all Rudolf Hess marches were banned.

will then attack police officers and smash windows at a McDonald's. The relationship between action and culture is complex and manifold. Music can help decode reality, heighten one's sense of belonging to a community, foster solidarity, and confirm one's conviction that the world is unjust and violent; it can also legitimize violence against the police and the redeeming riot. Some musicians perform at benefits for collectives working in solidarity with protesters[24] and on occasion march in demonstrations themselves. What's more, the counterculture environment of punk—and, for that matter, hip hop, techno, and electro—is permeated with violence. Punks are constantly harassed by the police, concerts are attacked by neo-Nazi skinheads, squatters who have taken over private property so that they can live in accordance with their own values are brutally evicted by the police, and so on. At times, protesters chanting song lyrics about riots have played on the ambiguity of calling for a riot while staging one only in words. This occurred at a demonstration held during the 2012 Quebec student strike. The crowd took up a slogan drawn from a song by the dada-punk group Mise en demeure, "Violence légitime, mon oeil" (legitimate violence, my eye). The song, which appears on the group's 2013 album *Il pleut des pavés* (It's Raining Paving Stones), was written in the wake of a demonstration where police used concussion grenades, costing one protester the use of an eye: "C'est pas les pacifiques qui vont changer l'histoire / on pitche des pavés, pis on brûle des chars" (it's not the pacifists who'll change history / we toss paving stones and we burn cars). In "La commune," the same band expressed the idea that throwing stones at bank windows is a way to express political ideas: "On a lancé des belles idées en forme de roches sur des vitrines" (we throw nice ideas in the form of rocks at the windows).

The festive aspect of rioting is underscored in the song "Petit agité" (restless kid), by Bérurier Noir, from their 1985 album *Concerts pour détraqués* (Concerts for the Deranged) (our translation):

Marked by hate
Youths on the rampage
Nothing to lose
Cars in flame
The projects burn
And madness prevails
Rebellious kids
Torch the trashcans
It's party time tonight.[25]

Étienne, who took part in political riots in Europe, explains: "The thing that strikes me at every riot is the jovial side of the vandalism. You get the impression people are celebrating ... They jump around and dance ... It's really exuberant, it's fun."[26] David Graeber, whose article "The New Anarchists" appeared in the *New Left Review*, states that "help[ing] to take down the security fence [at the Summit of the Americas in Quebec City] was certainly one of the most exhilarating experiences of my life."[27] And words such as "heady," "blissful," "orgasmic," and "intoxicating" (our translations) are recurrent in Clément Barette's interviews with French political rioters.

Some websites today are entirely dedicated to images and videos of riots. Activists visit these sites regularly, recommend and exchange URLs, and even gather on certain evenings—sometimes with an ample supply of alcohol—to watch the "best" riots on websites such as "The Ultimate Riot Collection" and "World Wide Riots."[28] The term "riot porn" has been used to express the excitement these images generate. Just as pornography offers "sexual scripts"—that is, ways of engaging in sexual relations—"riot porn" allows viewers to fantasize about one day imitating the rioters' on-camera performances. However, that term is problematic since it is an explicit reference to women's sexual exploitation. "Riot theatre" or "riot choreography" would be more appropriate.

Mass exultation of the kind captured in depictions of the French Revolution, and in images of the fall of the Berlin Wall 200 years later, is rooted in a particular social and political context. An affinity group of the Black Bloc in Genoa specifically stated that their direct action was not merely an "arena where violent individuals could blow off steam," since the targets were not chosen at random.[29] But another Black Blocker has said, "I think it's an expression of frustration, a way to let off steam for people who have understood that their interests are at odds with those of the institutions they are attacking."[30]

Regarding the police and the political-economic system, a Black Bloc participant in Quebec City in April 2001 stated:

> Direct action produces a kind of pleasure. Let me explain. True violence is the violence of state and capitalist oppression. The oppression is constantly visible. Every day we go by a McDonald's, which reminds us that exploitation exists. Some people are repeatedly harassed by the police. But at that point we are in a position of weakness. These situations of exploitation and oppression cause frustration, compelling us to look for an outlet, which is what vandalism provides.[31]

Stones and Molotov cocktails fly toward a police line in the Athenian neighbourhood of Exarchia, a stronghold for anti-authoritarians with a history of radical struggle, Athens, May 1, 2010.

For Paul, a French veteran of various political riots, collective confrontations with the police enable him to take "revenge": "State violence is a daily thing. It is not as concrete as the violence of rioting, but it is there, widespread, in the economic, social, institutional spheres, the police, and a majority of upstanding people. The riot is an act of total exasperation, a first response."[32]

Although Black Bloc actions are driven by emotions, they cannot be reduced to the stereotype of irrational young thugs blindly pursuing violence for the pure pleasure of trashing anything and everything. On the contrary, the emotions are rooted in a social context and a political experience. Direct action is a *reaction* to feelings of injustice and to situations of domination, inequality, and systemic violence.

The Quebec City demonstrations in April 2001 offered a young man from a disadvantaged neighbourhood who was constantly harassed by the police the opportunity to bring about a momentary shift in the power struggle and to shed the role of powerless victim. "I come from the suburbs and the cops do as they please there all year round and no one says a word," he explained. "Hitting a cop is not violence, it's vengeance."[33] Blunt statements such as this testify to the perception that the world is unjust and that everyday victims of police brutality, and of the economic and political system more generally, need redress. Here, emotion is at the core of action, but it is felt only in a specific economic and political context, and it is part of a more comprehensive consideration of tactics. Maxim Fortin, who examined the anti-capitalist movement's actions during the Summit of the Americas in Quebec City, notes in this regard:

> The factors compelling youths from poor neighbourhoods and ghettos to embrace the methods of the Black Blocs are relatively obvious: 1) they allow them to physically express their anger, be it toward the "system," the police, the rich, etc.; 2) they reduce the risk of being arrested, even though the penalty for those arrested will be harsh; 3) they make it possible to get hold of merchandise ordinarily beyond their means; 4) they enable them to protest without having to get involved in militant networks usually exogenous to their own social networks and dominated by "highly educated, white, middle-class activists" who are often in a position to devote time to more formal, organizational activism.[34]

Even in situations as violent as the one in Genoa in 2001, it is possible to express a poetics of freedom through a political riot. This is evident in the letter that one person protesting the legitimacy of the G8 Summit wrote to "mother" (presumably the writer's):

> Around this besieged fortress I was happy at times to enter spaces liberated through our efforts. I had an occasionally infinitesimal feeling of freedom as we opened the Zones of temporary autonomy,[35] the streets belonged to us for a few precious moments ...

There's no point in scolding me like a democrat, I broke only some
dishes, the house is unfortunately still standing.[36]

The Economy

The emotions felt in action can be explained by the economic and
political circumstances experienced by Black Bloc members and their
affinity groups, as well as by their shared anarchist analysis of the capitalist system. A French "anarcho-communist" who has taken part in
various demonstrations throughout Europe puts it this way: "I have
worked, and still do, in bars, on construction sites, in factories. There, I
see that my interests are not the same as the boss's. So there is a veritable social war: It's always those close to me—family, friends—who suf-
fer, always the same people who are victims every day, at work, etc."
In answer to the question, "Why carry out direct actions against the
system?", he says: "There are millions of reasons. Capitalism produces nothing but reasons to rise up against it. All capitalist production
causes pain; my own pleasure in this system brings suffering to others.
This world makes you puke, and the horrors you witness every day call
for a response."[37]

This discourse is clearly in line with anarchist critical analysis,
which describes capitalism as a fundamentally illegitimate system
because it rests on the authoritarian and non-egalitarian principle of
a hierarchical division between, on one hand, those who direct and
organize work and the production of goods and services and, on the
other, those whose job it is to produce them. Investors and owners
alone determine production and profits, while wage earners are sub-
ordinated to them and must submit to their decisions or quit and look
for a new job, where they will once again find themselves subject to
the will of their superiors in the hierarchy. In this economic framework, where the pursuit of profit matters more to the owners than
maintaining a safe work environment, many employees are injured
or even killed on the job. What is true on the micro level is also true
on the macro level. Owners prefer to accumulate profits rather than

concern themselves with the millions of people in Africa and elsewhere who, unable to afford life-saving drugs, are struck down by AIDS, or worry about the disastrous ecological effects of overproduction and hyper-consumerism. Furthermore, in a number of countries the champions of capitalism do not hesitate to threaten and kill people who are trying to defend workers' rights and dignity. Finally, capitalist globalization appears to be aggravating the inequalities within and between countries.[38]

For anarchists, the only legitimate economic system is one whose primary objective is to satisfy the fundamental needs of each individual and to allow producers to participate directly in decisions concerning production, the organization of work, and the distribution of any surpluses or profits.[39] Capitalism, by contrast, rests on the principle of the right to private property and the pursuit of unlimited profits to the detriment of the essential needs of the have-nots. The motto "Profits before life" aptly encapsulates the system's core principle.

Some on the left, instead of decrying the violence of the Black Blocs and their allies, point to the implacable violence of the prevailing economic and political system—that is, they contrast the minimal violence of the Black Blocs with the excessive violence of the system they are protesting. Jaggi Singh of CLAC in Montreal has never himself used force during a demonstration.[40] But a few weeks before the Quebec City Summit of the Americas in April 2001, in an interview with a Montreal weekly, he made this observation:

> Let's be clear: There will be some very violent people in Quebec City between April 20 and 22. They are well organized and highly motivated. They are the 34 heads of state of the Americas, who will be meeting behind a four-kilometre-long wall protected by thousands of police officers. We should target and oppose the institutional violence (poverty, genocide of native peoples, militarization, prisons, destruction of the environment) promoted by the American Free-trade Zone and the Summit of the Americas, rather than fall into the trap of isolating and marginalizing certain protest groups that practice direct action.[41]

Similarly, in their communiqués and interviews at least since Seattle, Black Blockers almost everywhere[42] have expressed the same position with regard to their actions as a protester did at the 2010 Toronto G20: "This isn't violence. This is vandalism against violent corporations. We did not hurt anybody. They [the corporations] are the ones hurting people."[43] An Italian activist stakes out the following rigorous ethical position:

> I have also participated in peaceful demonstrations, believing it was the right thing to do. Violence, it's worth pointing out, is not a constant, nor is it an amusement. For us, violence sometimes is purely a matter of necessity. It isn't, as some would have you believe, indiscriminate violence. On the contrary, it is meaningful violence. You can disapprove of our political practice, but you have to be stupid not to see that we use violence against material things and detest violence against people. The use of violence against material things and the rejection of violence against people characterize the Black Blocs' political practice all over the world. The objects at which our violence is directed are not undifferentiated; they are symbols of power.[44]

As for confrontations with the police, the "Manifeste du Carré noir" (Black Square Manifesto) declares: "We maintain that an individual with protective equipment who is prepared to violently strike other individuals simply because he was ordered to do so, momentarily forsakes his own immunity from violence."[45]

Of course, many on the left and even on the extreme left will disagree with such comments about violence. For example, in discussing the legitimacy of the Black Blocs, Chris Hedges—who, as noted earlier, likens them to a "cancer"—has stated: "I would classify violence as the destruction of property and vandalism, the shouting of insulting messages to the police, physical confrontations with the police. Those are very clear-cut acts of violence."[46] Yet the violence of protesters, negligible when compared to other political and economic forms of violence, has a primarily symbolic significance. According to Maxim Fortin,

Black Bloc anarchists generally justify the destruction of property on grounds that it attacks the legitimacy of the cherished symbols of consumerism, that it causes monetary losses for the targeted companies, that it restores the use value of things by denying their commercial value—I'm referring here to cases of pillaging—that it is the expression of a growing popular anger, and that it demonstrates the non-reformist, radical, and revolutionary nature of certain militant movements.[47]

The Swiss philosopher Nicolas Tavaglione affirms that by targeting private and public property, the Black Blocs force the elites to state what they value more, material goods or human life and liberty: "The riot puts us before a societal choice as old as Europe: freedom or security. Because they raise this question the Black Blocs are the best political philosophers of our times."[48] In addition, those who destroy consumer goods view the experience as a liberating one and thus as meaningful in and of itself. Étienne, for instance, finds it important to make a distinction: "In general, I don't 'steal.' I break, I smash— it's more gratifying."[49] Barrette writes that pillage, rather than mere destruction, enables the emergence of a "society of abundance lasting a few moments," in which it is possible to experience sharing and the joy of belonging to a solidary community.[50] Something that is far more restorative and satisfying than retail therapy!

Politics

Anarchism considers the liberal state, and the politicians and police officers involved in the major economic summits, just as illegitimate as the capitalist economic system itself. Illegitimate because the liberal state and the authority of politicians are founded on the illusion that the political will of the people can be represented, especially if they have the right to elect their leaders. Elections are in no way democratic, since they do not enable people to govern but only to choose the masters who will govern on their behalf. Anarchists, then, can relate to a passage in *The Social Contract* where Jean-Jacques Rousseau discusses elections in England: "The English people believes itself to be free; it is gravely mistaken; it is free only during the election of Members of Parliament; as soon as the Members are elected, the people is enslaved; it is nothing. In the brief moments of its freedom, the English people makes such a use of that freedom that it deserves to lose it."[51] For anarchists, whenever an individual or a group of individuals such as a political party is chosen to represent the will and interests of a whole community, the situation invariably evolves to the advantage of the representatives rather than to the benefit of the represented community. The simple fact of occupying a position of authority means that elected politicians have personal interests that do not coincide with those of the population they claim to represent. Experience shows, moreover, that political elites are often tied to, or directly belong to, economic and military elites. Popular sovereignty is therefore an innocent fiction at best, and at worst an intentional lie that justifies by means of an esoteric discourse the power of an elected aristocracy claiming to be democratic.

The anarchist theoretician and activist Voltairine de Cleyre, author of *Direct Action* (1912), stressed the importance of individual autonomy when she differentiated direct action from indirect action. Political action is "direct" when people act on their own behalf in the political arena, neither obeying a leader nor being represented by someone speaking or acting in their name. "Indirect" political action involves voting for individuals seeking office so that they can, in theory, act in the name of and for the good of their constituencies. Voters act only indirectly on the political scene, except when they vote for the person who will make decisions and take actions on their behalf. In de Cleyre's view, indirect action "destroys initiative, quenches the individual rebellious spirit, teaches people to rely on someone else to do for them what they should do for themselves."[52]

In any case, the economic elite and the political elite share the same world view. During the financial crisis that began in 2008, states withdrew hundreds of billions of dollars from public coffers (hence, from taxpayers' pockets) to keep afloat the very banks that through their speculative operations had created the crisis in the first place; meanwhile, international institutions have demanded that the governments

A Black Bloc at an anti-austerity protest in front of the Greek Parliament, Athens, October 3, 2012.

of insolvent states (such as Greece and Spain) enact austerity policies. For the affected populations, this has meant reduced public services, lower wages, unemployment, and, subsequently, evictions and foreclosures. Thus, it is not that surprising that in recent years, Black Blocs have appeared in countries destabilized by major economic and financial crises as well as by austerity measures imposed on the people by the political elite.

Whatever its egalitarian discourse, the liberal state remains organized along authoritarian and hierarchical lines. The major economic summits epitomize this as well as the illegitimacy and violence of the state: a clique of politicians discuss the fate of the planet behind closed doors, protected by thousands of heavily armed police who forcefully drive away citizens denouncing the undemocratic nature of the process of making political decisions that affect everyone. A direct action may end in a confrontation with the police, but at least it enables some individuals to escape, for the brief duration of a riot, from a perpetual position of domination. Didier, from France, had this to say about a political riot in which he had participated: "It was the first time that power was not something above me. It was there, in front of me."[53]

Black Blockers repeatedly stress the distinction between the illegitimate, violent dynamic of the state and what is involved in their own actions. Katy, who was involved in several political riots in Europe, says that "violence ... is the police truncheon, enforced employment, hunger, war—that is violence, and it is not something I wish to use."[54] A man who joined in the Quebec City Black Bloc declares: "I am a pacifist, a non-violent activist, that is, I dream of a world without violence." Then he adds: "But we currently live in a violent, non-pacifist world, so I consider it legitimate for me to use force so as not to leave the state with a monopoly on violence, and because pacifist civil disobedience only results in a power relationship of victimization, because you let the police attack you, arrest you, put you on file." He then draws the surprising conclusion that if "the state has no choice but to use violence, then the state leaves us no choice but to use violence against it. It's the state, by being what it is, that created the Black Blocs."[55]

The philosopher Nicolas Tavaglione suggests that we take seriously

> the widespread hypothesis that the Black Blocs are anarchists. They mistrust the state and all forms of protest that involve collaboration with the forces of order. More fundamentally, they may adhere to an *ethical anarchism*: any form of power is humiliating because incompatible with the dignity of whoever is subject to it, and there is no moral obligation to obey the government. Or to a *political anarchism*: not only is all government predatory, but in addition the modern bureaucratic state is a castrating entity. Or even to a *social anarchism*: property, guaranteed by a robber state, is a form of theft; the labour market, where I must sell myself, is a form of rape.[56]

For the men and women who engage in them, the skirmishes that arise during large demonstrations are micro-revolutions through which it is possible, at the risk of bodily harm, to liberate the space (the street) and the time (a few hours) needed for a brief but powerful political experience outside the norms set by both the state and the leaders of the major political organizations. Though calls for global revolution may be pretentious, direct actions change our way of seeing our relationship to the city, to property, and to politics. Direct actions also allow the Black Blocs and their allies to signal their dissent and to partake in the old tradition of the right and duty to resist illegitimate authority.[57]

CHAPTER 4

CRITICISM OF THE BLACK BLOC: (UN)FRIENDLY FIRE

The Black Bloc tactic has many advantages, but it is also undermined by some significant shortcomings, so a number of apparently well-intentioned criticisms coming from the left and far left are worth considering. Specifically, Black Blocs are accused of fetishizing their own violence; of practising a sexist form of action, one that favours men while excluding women; and, finally, of antagonizing the working class and of drawing attention away from the legitimate demands of major non-violent social movements.

Fetishism

"Fetishism" refers to the notion that the use of force is a "pure" form of radical activism, politically superior to other types. The Black Blocs are threatened internally by the tendency for far left circles to develop a "radical" hard core to which individuals gain admittance—as well as an aura of "purity"—by "serving in battle." This process resembles in some ways a religious initiation: an individual strives to display and affirm a political identity whose purity depends on the execution of prescribed ritual acts, such as highly visible confrontations with the police, which are valorized in and of themselves, regardless of their political impact.

Violent direct action becomes a means for a would-be militant to affirm his or her political identity in the eyes of other militants. This makes it very tempting for that person to look down on and exclude those who do not equate radicalism with violence.[1] Here, anarchists behave no differently from the adherents of other ideologies: they resort to lofty principles—liberty, equality, justice, and so on—to rationalize their thirst for violence, prestige, and power. Indeed, anarchists have sometimes exploited the same arguments as liberal politicians or representatives of the armed forces who claim to be waging war in the name of "liberty" and "peace."

Many anarchists are aware of the dangers of fetishizing violence and stress the importance of not equating it with radicalism. A participant in the Quebec City Black Blocs asserts: "I have no patience with dogmatic pacifism, but there is also dogmatic violence, which sees violence as the one and only means to wage the struggle."[2] Another Black Blocker adds that it is a mistake to believe that "the demo is the ultimate political thing or that rioting necessarily means you're radical."[3] This outlook, voiced by North Americans, is shared by French activists like Didier, who points out that a demonstration is not a goal in itself, nor is it the only available political practice: "What I do is different! Political commitment just for the 'speed' and pleasure it brings you is worthless."[4] Finally, Sofiane, who has resorted to force in demonstrations, notes: "We don't advocate violence; it's not a program ... Because you can easily acquire a taste for violence, you get used to it ... But when it comes to doing militant work, not many people show up."[5]

A member of the Confédération nationale du travail (CNT)—a revolutionary, anarchist-identified labour union—who went to Genoa with a group of 15 young activists, framed the issue in these terms: "The point was to plunge [the young activists] into a truly tense situation, where they would have to deal with their adrenaline and understand how it works. For militants, militants who, in addition, claim to be revolutionary, this sort of situation is important ... What's more, to feel that you showed some 'mettle,' that's important."[6] Here, violence plays a part in the simultaneous construction of two identities: an anarchist identity, associated with an ethic of violent struggle, and the warrior identity, associated with a macho ethic whereby a man must learn to control his adrenalin and fight with honour.

Yet this attitude can lead quickly to disillusionment. A decade after participating in several Black Blocs, including one in Genoa in 2001, a veteran activist drew the following conclusion:

> The Black Bloc in Genoa was pathetic, as it was easily routed by some fifty police officers. It split into two groups: one dashed off and attacked a prison and a supermarket, the other fell back with the Tute Bianche. I was in the second group. We quickly changed our clothes, switching from black to the T-shirts of the Greens, for instance, and began smashing windows, with some members of the Tute Bianche following suit. From a military perspective, the Black Blocs in those days were pathetic because they didn't really suc-ceed in holding the street in the face of the police. So it was a mar-ginal, almost insignificant phenomenon.[7]

Fetishization of the Black Bloc also explains the discomfort that many *Autonomen* in Berlin feel with regard to the "activism tourists" who show up every May Day having no ties with the local militant net-work, wishing only to take part in a "big" Black Bloc and a "nice" riot, and giving no thought to what this action signifies for the community.

A related consequence has been the emergence of a "Black Bloc spectator" phenomenon—more specifically, demonstrators dressed in black who join the Black Bloc but slip away at the first signs of trouble. The Black Blockers who do not break ranks subsequently find them-selves caught off guard. As was noted in an Internet communiqué: "People who are afraid of heights obviously should not join an affin-ity group that hangs banners from the tops of buildings. By the same token, if someone is not prepared to assume, if necessary, at least one of the functions that the members of a Black Bloc expect to see fulfilled, it is probably not a good idea for that individual to join."[8]

Denunciations of the Black Blocs have also referred to "summit hopping." This sort of militant tourism is often viewed as not being con-ducive to a revolutionary perspective, and as leading instead to purely symbolic responses to the demonstrations of power that the summits embody.[9] What is worse, rioting at these events has become ritualized, with the two parties—the Black Bloc and the police—replaying the same roles on stages that vary little from one summit to the next. This is something that annoys the anarchist activist and writer Randall Amster[10] and the political philosopher John Holloway.[11] For their part, David Tough[12] and Naggh severely condemn "the local riot ... that goes hand in hand with 'alterglobalization' ideology":

> There, we see riot activists moving about and fighting in cities where they are viewed as invaders and strangers, and where, despite two or three attempts each year, they never succeed in rallying the local poor, who are quite disgusted with the phoney rages they have no part in. This riot tourism, easily planned and staged for the enemy, has the advantage of venting frustrations ... and presenting a tailor-made image of the riot, that is, unattractive, sad, sinister, and hopeless. Because these matches, in cities completely locked down by the police, are not the kind whose outcome keeps us in suspense.[13]

This discourse, which runs through the whole anarchist tradition, consists in denouncing everything that does not appear to maximize the revolutionary potential of a situation. It is an attitude found even within the Black Blocs, some of whose members like to believe that a violent demonstration opens up revolutionary perspectives. Fortunately, a large number of Black Blockers adopt a more realistic outlook. The unnamed author of the preface to the *Black Bloc Papers* put it this way: "I'm not saying that the Bloc will end the world's problems. I am, however, certain that physically confronting authorities which physically uphold a rotten system and reminding the rest of the populace that such things can be done is healthy."[14]

In sum, many activists who apply this tactic are fully aware of its limitations. They do not believe that the great rising will take place when they turn the next corner,[15] and they may even admit to moments of pessimism about the possibility of a global revolution.[16] A Québécoise woman who participated in several Black Blocs lamented: "We are in a period when there is no possibility of a revolution." Then she added: "We do what we can to radicalize the debate and to reach people so a more radical politicization can come about."[17] A resident of Strasbourg, France, with many demonstrations to his credit and no illusions about the great rising, affirms that "I am an 'insurgent in search of an insurrection,' to borrow an phrase from the movement of the unemployed. [That means] taking action against the expulsion of a refugee or helping a family whose electricity has been cut off; responding with outrage to the death of a protester, to the repression of a whole people."[18] In fact, there are many anarchists—Black Blockers and others—whose primary objective is not to bring about the revolution but rather to convince the greatest number of individuals of the relevance of anarchism, or to strengthen the anarchist movement. Or it is to help people take control of their lives, develop a sense of community solidarity, mobilize to resist the various systems of domination, and work to improve the living conditions of underprivileged groups, here and now.[19]

Sexism

"We're here! We're queer! We're anarchists! We'll fuck you up!",[20] chanted the Black Bloc during the Pittsburgh G20 Summit in 2009, implying that the Black Blocs' aesthetic statement makes it possible to mask gender identities and erase sexual differences. "You can't do gender in a riot," claims A.K. Thompson, author of *Black Bloc White Riot*.[21] Indeed, when observing a demonstration or riot, whether in person or in photos and videos, how can anyone discern the sex of a stone-throwing Black Blocker? Echoing the words of Mary Black,[22] a member of the Black Bloc in Genoa in 2001, Krystalline Kraus, writing in 2002, commented on her experience in Canada:

"Blocking up" to become the Black Bloc is a great equalizer. With everyone looking the same—everyone's hair tucked away, our faces obscured by masks, I'm nothing less and nothing more than one entity moving with the whole. Everyone is capable of the same. And the politics of "nice girls don't throw stones" is suspended, and I'm free to act outside of the traditional "serve tea, not Molotov cocktails" rules. It's once the mask comes off, the problems begin . . . Sure, women are gaining popular ground in the movement, but some topics are still taboo for us. And with machismo still ruling the streets—especially during a riot—what women have to say, often gets lost in the tear gas fog.[23]

Many critics of Black Blocs have contended that this type of brutal action partakes of a macho mystique and does not encourage women to join in.[24] Others suggest that expressions of anger through destruction simply confirm and amplify aggressive masculinity.[25] Addressing themselves to women and men in militant networks, some feminists have denounced men's monopolizing of Black Blocs and encouraged women to take part in them. For example, to articulate their desire for inclusion and diversity in this type of collective action, *Tute Nere*, a group of Italian revolutionary feminists, came up with the slogan "Black Bloc—not only for your boyfriend!"

Thus, the question of women in the Black Blocs is complex, particularly if it is framed in terms of sexual and gender identities. In Germany, women belonging to queer communities are generally reluctant to join Black Blocs, which they see as the incarnation of a macho-style activism; women in the anti-fascist networks participate in greater numbers. There is an apparent paradox at work here, given that the queer movement aims in principle to deconstruct conventional sexual and gender identities. One might expect queer women to be attracted to a militant practice commonly identified as masculine; yet they are more reticent about joining Black Blocs. Conversely, female anti-fascist militants, who, unlike queer women, may not propose to upset the order of gender identities, are more likely to take part in a Black Bloc. Perhaps because they work in a macho-style activist environment, getting involved in this sort of action—whether they are heterosexual, bisexual, or lesbian—has the advantage of bringing recognition from male comrades.[26]

Meanwhile, *Women in the Black Bloc*, a communiqué from the Black Women Movement (BWM) based in the United States, criticizes activists who consider women fundamentally passive and demands acknowledgment that it is possible for women to use political force: "It is up to us to remind those who doubt our ability and strength that we are just as capable. We can be tender, so can men, we can smash a window, so can men, we can cry, so can men, we can throw a brick, so can men."[27] Recall here that historically, women have often participated in riots to protest a political or economic system or to demand their rights, and that feminist groups such as the Wimmin's Fire Brigade in Vancouver and *Rote Zora* in Germany have firebombed sex trade businesses to express their opposition to the economic and sexual exploitation of women.[28]

A statement by a small group of activists in Boston asked its readers to "support direct action and the Black Bloc as a tactic for empowerment," while at the same time denouncing "Manarchy," that is, "aggressive, competitive behavior within the anarchist movement that is frighteningly reminiscent of historically oppressive male gender roles." Two of the statement's authors reported that at a meeting to plan a Black Bloc in a forthcoming protest, "one man declared: 'If you're not willing to take

In 1989, feminist writer Ingrid Strobl was arrested for supporting the Revolutionary Cells and Red Zora. This February 1989 solidarity demonstration in Essen, Germany, was attacked by police.

a hit [to the head with a baton] and you're not willing to go to jail, don't march with the Black Bloc.'" But the authors' statement went on to say:

> We also understand that people in different situations have different needs. In other words, not everyone can and wants to get beat up and sent to jail for an act that may or may not be perceived as tactically useful ... For example, as four white, college students, it's pretty easy for us to be militants at mass actions. In addition to easy access to lawyers, the cops and courts treat us better than classes of people who are traditionally victimized. It is much harder for people of color, the economically disadvantaged, and people who are not physically capable of intense physical confrontation to take such a position ... We are not the Navy Seals. We are not heroes. We are anarchists, building a space that is empowering, accepting, inclusive, accessible, communicative, and community oriented.[29]

Yet male activists on the far left, be they anarchists, communists, or environmentalists, have made very little effort, beyond fine words, to abandon their privileges as members of the dominant male class, even within the Black Blocs. In spite of anarchists' avowed adherence to principles of freedom and equality, Black Blocs have been known to reproduce a sexual division of tasks. A woman who took part in several Black Blocs during the Quebec student strike of 2012 observed that women did the shopping, for example, when fabric was needed to make flags and banners.[30] More than a decade earlier, during a meeting to prepare a Black Bloc in Montreal, the men ended up in the backyard of an apartment honing their slingshot skills while the women were in the kitchen making Molotov cocktails.[31] A woman who had joined various Black Blocs in Quebec deplored the fact that "inside the anarchist movement there is prestige attached to being on the front line, taking part in the confrontation, breaking windows. I find this unfortunate, because there are lots of other people doing lots of other things that are just as important."[32] Her own participation in Black Blocs involved reconnaissance and surveillance missions. She noted that less value was attached to this work than to direct confrontations with the police.

It seems that women's participation in Black Bloc actions is greater during the organizational work preceding them than during the actual confrontations on the ground. This, however, depends on the particular activist network. There are no doubt a few small Black Blocs where women are completely absent, but elsewhere they sometimes represent half the contingent,[33] while some Black Bloc affinity groups are composed mainly or exclusively of women.[34]

The situation varies with the context and the specific event. In 2000, an activist who had been part of a Black Bloc in Washington, D.C., during a march against the IMF and the World Bank estimated that about half its members were women and that the Bloc was not ethnically homogeneous. She concluded that "the Black Bloc may have been more diverse than the mobilization as a whole."[35] Vittorio Sergi, an Italian activist who participated in the Europe-wide co-ordination of mobilizations against the 2007 G8 Summit in Rostock, observes that there are more women in Black Blocs in Germany than in Italy.[36] In Canada, there were fewer women in the Black Blocs in the early 2000s but many more toward 2010, during the protests against the Olympic Games in Vancouver and the Toronto G20, where—it is worth pointing out—they were not restricted to logistics, support, and first aid. During the Quebec student strike in 2012, female Black Blockers were often quicker than their male counterparts to graffiti the walls and to break the windows of banks and army recruiting centres.

There is no easy explanation for the place of women in the Black Blocs, but some hypotheses are worth considering, despite their shortcomings. It seems that the number of women Black Blockers is higher in places where feminism—radical feminism in particular—is more robust, such as Germany and Quebec, than in France or Italy, for example. In Montreal, anarchist networks include a very high proportion of women; among the visitors at the 2012 Anarchist Book Fair in Montreal, for example, women represented roughly 60 percent. Finally, because women are discriminated against and, on the whole, poorer than men under capitalism, it should come as no surprise that a great many of them feel anger toward banks and international corporations.

During the 2010 G20 protest in Toronto, Black Blockers smashed the windows of an American Apparel store and even threw feces at the mannequins. As one woman Black Blocker explained about women in Black Blocs: "Obviously, they are more sensitive to targets associated with patriarchy, such as shop windows displaying sexist advertisements."

Still, one woman who joined a number of Black Blocs over the course of the prolonged social conflict in Quebec regards the Black Bloc as "a boys' club." Women were initially admitted because of "a relationship with a man, either a boyfriend or a lover." She notes, however, that in the end a large number of women joined Black Blocs during the student strike and estimates that 80 percent of them were in all-female affinity groups. In her view, women's actions "are more thorough, more successful"; also, their "relationship with the target is more thought out" so that they sometimes acknowledge that the most reasonable choice is "to forget a particular target." She adds: "Many women hear the call of the brick, but not anytime, anyhow." Obviously, they are more sensitive to targets associated with patriarchy, such as

*An all-women Black Bloc during the 2012 Montreal May Day
demonstration in Montreal.*

shop windows displaying sexist advertisements. Finally, women "are
more mindful of the other members of the group" and "don't leave
anyone behind when people scatter and run."[37]

This testimony is borne out by that of another woman who joined
various Black Blocs during the Quebec student strike, though in a different network. She identifies herself as anarchist and queer rather
than feminist. According to her, women accounted for between 60 and
70 percent of Black Bloc membership during the conflict. Also, she preferred to plan and carry out actions only with women, because "the
plans are less formal, less controlled":

> We talk more and generally leave more room for living the moment.
> There are fewer preconceptions of what we aim to accomplish and
> more discussion of how to go about it. We stick together and there's
> much more communication when decisions are being made in the
> street. Men are more individualistic. They don't feel obliged to

come back to the group and can take off without warning. It's "My top priority is me!" I call them "lone wolves," whereas women form wolf packs."[38]

Thus, the Black Blocs can be a space where there is not always a clear distinction between masculine and feminine (whatever those terms mean), or between what is "efficient" and what is not. It is therefore possible with such collective action to challenge conventional sexual identities, and to demonstrate that there is not necessarily a contradiction between fighting and co-operating, or between caring and being violent.

Yet other women Black Blockers also expressed concerns, such as the anonymous author of the letter *Après avoir tout brûlé* (*After Having Burnt Everything*), who participated in several Black Blocs in Europe, including the one in Strasbourg against the NATO Summit in 2009. She complained about the "petty macho dog-fights" between male activists who were trying to "impose the hierarchy of the day": "As a woman in our milieu, I worked hard to earn my stripes, to say the right things, to show my mettle to others and to myself by regularly taking part in skirmishes ... Violence, whoever uses it, has consequences on emotional 'health' ... I have no sympathy for pacifism as an ideology. But we need to help each other to fight with determination over the long term and to stay healthy individually and collectively."[39]

Moreover, female activism does not prevent misogyny and sexist behaviour, including harassment and even sexual assault. Regrettably, both occurred in radical and anarchist networks during the Quebec student strike of 2012. The anonymity provided by black clothing allowed a man who had sexually assaulted women activists to join a protest, until some of his former comrades recognized him despite the mask, and kicked him out of the crowd. Similar incidents had occurred during the 2003 EU Summit, when anarchists occupied Aristotle University in Thessaloniki,[40] and during the mobilizations in Seattle and Quebec City in 1999 and 2001 respectively.[41]

Anarchists are usually very quick to denounce police brutality and violence against activists or "ordinary" citizens, or neo-Nazis assaulting people of colour, yet they seem far more hesitant when female militants are abused by their male counterparts. Referring specifically to the Black Bloc tactic, T-Bone Kneegrabber notes:

> You can easily round up 500 black clad anarchists to fuck shit up at a frat house where rapists live, but someone points a finger at a "progressive" man and all of a sudden there's a process; all of a sudden she [the survivor] is being divisive ... We, as "anarchists," hold a society (that we do not have faith in) to a higher standard than we hold our friends to! ... Just because a man identifies as radical, does not make him an angel.[42]

In 2013 in Egypt, most of the Black Bloc participants apparently were men, though some women may have been directly involved. In the words of one observer, "when women were being brutally attacked [by state-backed 'rape squads'] in Tahrir Square ... beyond the ability of groups like Operation Anti-Sexual Harassment to protect them, Black Bloc activists literally appeared out of nowhere to take on the often armed groups of attackers and protect the women and other activists."[43]

The Politics of Criticism

According to many activists in progressive movements, including the anti-austerity, Occupy, and alter-globalization movements, the greatest drawback of the Black Bloc tactic is that it prevents the public and the elites from hearing the legitimate messages of progressive organizations. The police themselves use this argument to undercut the legitimacy of Black Blocs, as indicated in a statement by Toronto police chief William Blair, extracted here from a review conducted by the Toronto Police Service in the aftermath of the 2010 G20 Summit: "Last June, we saw levels of violence we had never seen before in Toronto. People came to the G20 Summit, not to engage in debate or discussion or demonstration, but to infiltrate lawful, peaceful protests, and use them as cover to commit vandalism and violence."[44] This apparently commonsensical outlook also finds expression in letters to the editor, such as those concerning the student strike in Quebec: "The students need to wake up and realize that letting the Black Bloc and other anarchists or masked vandals infiltrate their ranks does nothing to advance their cause."[45]

It is very common for mainstream journalists to take up and disseminate this sort of censure. During the 2010 G20 Summit in Toronto, for example, a *Toronto Sun* reporter wrote that "legitimate protesters who work within the law, who attempt to get their voices heard through less controversial means, may feel that their concerns won't be heard above the chaos." He then quoted Ella Kokotsis, director of external relations of the University of Toronto's G8 and G20 Research Group: "When this kind of thing happens, it just diverts the entire world's attention to what's going on in the streets [and] takes away from what G8 leaders have done."[46] Interestingly, another article in the same newspaper was subtitled, "Prime minister boasts of G8's success, vows to carry on meetings, *but not much is accomplished*"[47] (not a surprising result, given that the German chancellor and the British prime minister took time out to watch a World Cup soccer match[48]). Almost ten years earlier, an Agence France-Presse (AFP) journalist covering the G8 Summit in Genoa had quoted German Chancellor Gerhard Schröder as saying, "it should be acknowledged that due to a few hundred or a few thousand violent protestors, the cause of those concerned with the consequences of globalization who demonstrated peacefully was *completely discredited*."[49] The German chancellor did not indicate how the G8 decision makers' actions would have been in any way different had there been no riot. Would they have, then, taken seriously the concerns of those who demonstrated peacefully? And why do a few Black Blockers have the power—by smashing some windows—to divert the G8 leaders' minds from important concerns about globalization?

Journalists do not hesitate to amplify this theme. "Antiglobalization will not survive with any credibility unless it breaks with these infiltrated vandals," wrote an AFP reporter, commenting on an article in Madrid's *El Mundo*.[50] This is a recurrent idea. After the 2012 May Day demonstration in Seattle, where the Black Bloc smashed several windows (Wells Fargo, Starbucks, the Federal Court building), a *Seattle*

Weekly blogger commented: "The organized speeches on police brutality, immigration, social justice and capitalism went mostly unheard by the public watching and reading yesterday's and today's media reports: most coverage was in-depth windows-breaking news"[51] (a point illustrated, actually, by this very blog post). A few weeks later, a reporter at the *Los Angeles Times* chimed in, using the same terms, once again without discussing precisely the issues that the Black Blocs' actions must not be allowed to eclipse: "Their antics stole attention from the thousands of peaceful protesters who may have had serious things to say about the expanding divide between rich and poor."[52] Editorialists, reporters, and columnists have been chanting this same mantra for over ten years. In 2001, for instance, after the EU Summit in Göteborg, Laurent Zecchini of *Le Monde* concluded straight away that "the danger, of course, is that being lumped together [with the vandals] obscures the message of a 'civil society' whose legitimate concerns are drowned in the fury of the confrontations."[53] There is something rather ironic in the stance taken by media professionals like these: they could very well choose *not* to cover the "violence" and to focus instead on the "real issues," if those issues truly mattered for them, instead of berating the "vandals" for diverting the attention of the media (including themselves).

Furthermore, the media relay the assessments of the reformist movement's spokespersons, such as C. Hutchinson, an activist in the British group Drop the Debt, who opined: "We don't want the movement to stop because there is too much violence. We need peaceful demonstrations so we can get across our messages."[54] Significantly, Fabien Lefrançois, of the French group Agir ici, allowed that the Black Blocs' rough stuff had apparently produced such a shock wave that it helped reformists "force negotiations to get underway, open debates, and be heard." But he also noted: "It's true, the violent actions of the Black Blocs served *our* purpose at a certain point in time ... But they can do *us* a disservice in the long run."[55] According to the head of the French section of Greenpeace, Bruno Rebelle, "*our* work is discredited by this violence."[56] The message of the progressive elite is crystal clear: its work should be the priority, and the radicals had better calm down, toe the line, and behave themselves. Susan George, vice-president of ATTAC-France, has taken up the same refrain: "Because of a few unmanageable idiots, we come across as simpleminded anticapitalists and violent anti-Europeans."[57] Referring to the EU Summit in Göteborg in June 2001, she lamented that the street actions had drawn the public's attention away from a televised debate involving European politicians and seven representatives of the movement, including herself.

Even peaceful demonstrations are often reduced to a few anecdotal images.[58] Concerning the alter-globalization movement, for instance, French journalists have repeatedly used the expression "bon enfant" (friendly, good-natured) to describe peaceful demonstrations, highlighting the innocuous aspects of these events.[59] In a TF1 news report from Genoa on July 18, 2001, the atmosphere at the demonstrators' headquarters was described as "good-natured"; in the next day's report, the term "techno-parade" was used to describe the first demonstration in that city, a non-violent event. In December 2000, a journalist for the Paris daily *Libération* referred to peaceful actions carried out in Nice, where the EU Summit was under way, as "antiglobalization folklore": "The Spaniards brought out their drums, the Catalans their fifes, and the Galicians their bagpipes." It was a "festive happening" during which dozens of activists jumped into the Baie des Anges. A nine-metre-long "financial shark" that was supposed to have travelled from Marseille to intrude on the bathers never arrived. The article continued: "'He got deflated,' one swimmer quipped." With the subtitles "Bagpipes" and "Deflated shark," the article eschewed all political references.[60] Only rarely is the political significance of demonstrations, violent or not, taken seriously by the mainstream media.

The fact is, the mass media are eager to cover the spectacle provided by "rioters," and they generally give a higher priority to a "violent" demonstration than to a calm, "friendly" march. I can attest to this personally, having served several times as a guest analyst and commentator for RDI, Radio-Canada's 24-hour French-language TV news network, when it was covering alter-globalization demonstrations. During production meetings, decisions on the placement of cameras and vehicles were based in part on the potential for "vandalism."

Thus, a correlation developed between the media's coverage of alter-globalization demonstrations and the direct actions of the Black Blocs. By way of illustration, the marches held in November 2001 against the IMF, the World Bank, and the G20 Summit in Ottawa, and then in January–February 2002 against the World Economic Forum in New York, were referred to as "non-events" by members of the teams I was a part of, precisely because not enough havoc was generated at those events to satisfy a certain audience. Six months later, in the absence of any violence despite the participation of a small Black Bloc, the G8 Summit in Calgary presented the same problem for the society of the spectacle.

The media hope to capture scenes of violence, which for them are highly profitable.[61] They have been far more attentive to alter-globalization demonstrations since Seattle *because of* the presence of Black Blocs; as a result, they have also been more attentive to the alter-globalization discourses. The participants in the Black Blocs are

Photographers scramble for a closer shot of a burning police car at the Toronto G20 Summit protest, June 2010.

Photograph by Andy K. Bond. Reproduced by permission of the photographer.

fully aware of this dynamic and have often asserted that their actions draw media attention to mobilizations and rallies, that they "[spark] discussions and debates, [get] people to take a position; whether or not they are for or against this kind of action hardly matters to us, because we know why we do it."[62] Indeed, the possibility that Black Blocs and their allies will carry out sensational actions has enabled the movement for some years to remain highly newsworthy. Scholars who have systematically analyzed the relationship between the media and violent demonstrations concur that the use of force helps generate significant media coverage, at least initially (though when violent demonstrations become routine, media interest may fade).[63] These scholars do not agree, however, when it comes to determining whether recourse to violence has a positive or negative effect on media coverage.

The attitude of mainstream journalists toward violence depends greatly on who is employing it. They are generally quite tolerant when violence is used by local police forces or by the country's own military, or that of allies. Their tolerance stays relatively high with regard to "respectable" protesters, such as students in a foreign country demonstrating against an authoritarian regime, or homegrown, middle-class trade unionists. Usually, though, they condemn the violence of "others"—police and military personnel of enemy states, "suburban youths," Black Blockers. This condemnation is expressed through pejorative labels—"young extremists," "brutes," "thugs," and so on—and in almost total silence with regard to their political motives.

Antagonizing Public Opinion and the Working Class

Given this media environment, it seems logical to expect the Black Blocs' use of force during demonstrations to damage the protest movement's public image. At best, they attract the attention of the cameras, but the resulting media coverage never portrays them in a sympathetic light. Yet this implies a homogeneous movement, one from which the Black Bloc is excluded. It also implies that "public opinion" is uniform. Chris Samuel analyzed the Black Bloc tactic in the light of the 2010 Toronto G20 Summit; he concluded that "activist attempts to impose a new definition of violence or even to open up the question of violence in the minds of the watching public" were doomed to fail because the Black Bloc lacked "sufficient symbolic" power "to impose a new definition" of violence on a "neoliberal public." The assumption here is that a few hundred activists breaking windows in downtown Toronto were convinced their action on its own had the "power to modify conscious beliefs about property and its relation to capitalist exploitation"; and, furthermore, that "the public" is of one mind.[64] In reality, however, civil society and public opinion are heterogeneous. As a member of the Black Bloc in London during the "anti-cuts" demonstrations asserted: "We are not in any way setting out to terrorise the public. We *are* the public."[65] A Canadian woman and veteran Black Blocker was asked: "How would you respond to those who say the Black Blocs give a poor image of the antiglobalization movement as a whole?" Her reply: "Whose image? I think the assumption is that people are not inspired by rebellion. And also that the audience is white and middle-class."[66]

It would be more accurate to speak of civil *societies* and public *opinions.* Some public opinions judge the actions of the Black Blocs and their allies harshly. But there are also those who feel inadequately represented by progressive organizations, which they believe hamper the movement against capitalist globalization and impede social justice; these people look positively on Black Bloc actions and perceive them as politically significant. Of course, this analysis of public opinion is not shared by the detractors of the Black Blocs, such as Mario Roy, an editorialist for Montreal's *La Presse.* In late July 2003, after demonstrations against the WTO in Montreal, he penned this reductive assessment: "Vandalism ... is abysmally stupid and perceived as such by the *entire* population."[67] Sweeping generalizations like this ignore the existence of independent media networks—independent radio stations and print and Internet publications—and the punk and hip hop countercultures, among others, all of which abound with far more nuanced debates about Black Bloc actions than can be found in the mainstream media.

Lynn Owens and L. Kendall Palmer studied the after-effects of the media's coverage of Black Bloc actions in Seattle, and found that it boosted public interest in anarchism. They identified a threefold dynamic: (1) The mainstream media gave the Black Blocs a very high profile, but a negative one, presenting them as the embodiment of anarchy, in the sense of chaos and violence. (2) The media attention generated a marked increase in the number of visits to anarchist Internet sites, including those (such as news.infoshop.org) providing information and forums for discussions on the Black Blocs. (3) The mainstream media subsequently showed more interest in other facets of anarchism, such as anarchist soccer leagues, book fairs, and so on; meanwhile, stories about the Black Blocs sometimes included one or two texts (often based on anarchist Internet sites) explaining their motives and political rationale or dealing with a range of topics.[68] So it happened that during the Quebec student strike of 2012, after months of demonstrations with an ongoing Black Bloc presence, the Montreal Anarchist Book Fair, held in May of the same year, saw a considerable rise in the number of visitors, who were curious to learn more about anarchism. Sales of books, especially introductions to the subject (including this one, in its earlier French edition), increased significantly.

It seems that within the alter-globalization movement, many activists and protesters do not reject political violence, and thus are not necessarily disturbed by the Black Bloc. During the 2012 Quebec student strike, a protester expressed to a journalist his opinion of the anarchists who were smashing bank windows and battling the police: "I never threw anything, I never smashed anything, but I am with them. I am a *casseur* in my heart."[69] Even the American eco-feminist Starhawk, a hard core pacifist, declared: "I like the Black Bloc ... In general, I think breaking windows and fighting cops in a mass action is counterproductive [but the participants in the Black Bloc] are my comrades and allies in this struggle and ... we need room in this movement for rage, for impatience, for militant fervor."[70] Donatella della Porta and Sidney Tarrow, two analysts of social movements, interviewed some 800 protesters during the G8 Summit in Genoa in 2001 and found that only 41 percent of them were prepared to condemn all forms of violence.[71] At the demonstrations against the G8 Summit in Évian in June 2003, 16.7 percent of the protesters stated that damaging property can be "effective," 40 percent thought that physically resisting the police can be "effective," and over 66 percent said that they themselves had physically resisted the police at some point or were prepared to do so.[72]

Yet the leaders of progressive organizations, hoping above all to mobilize the trade unions, are still not convinced of the usefulness of Black Bloc actions.[73] Susan George, for her part, points an accusing finger at the Black Blockers in Genoa in 2001 for acting irresponsibly toward others:

> Are you happy, protesters? ... you, the genuine Black Blockers, who never participated in any of the preparatory meetings that went on for months, who don't belong to any of the 700 responsible Italian organizations that had decided democratically to practice creative and active non-violence. Are you happy with your unilateral actions, to have infiltrated groups of peaceful demonstrators so that they too got gassed and clubbed ... ? Are you happy we've finally got our martyr? His name was Carlo Giuliani. ... A man has died. If we can't guarantee peaceful, creative demonstrations, workers and official trade unions won't join us.[74]

The implication, then, is that a demonstration is a kind of private space—a view embraced wholeheartedly by an editor of *Rouge*, the organ of the LCR, who accuses the Black Blocs "of *squatting* demonstrations and obliging them to take on a type of confrontation that they do not want."[75] Such allegations, however, fail to mention that many Black Blockers are also involved in mobilization campaigns and that the demonstrations they take part in are organized in the main by radical groups. Yet even some on the far left and in the anarchist movement assume that the Black Blocs alienate the "working class"[76] with their clothing and lifestyle choices, which are associated with the anarchist counterculture (which is stronger in Germany and North America than in France or Greece).[77] For insurrectionary anarchists, such distinctions are specious and conceal a form of political manipulation:

> We are of the exploited and excluded, and thus our task is to act. Yet some critique all action that is not part of a large and visible

social movement as "acting in the place of the proletariat." They counsel analysis and waiting, instead of acting. Supposedly, we are not exploited alongside the exploited; our desires, our rage and our weaknesses are not part of the class struggle. This is nothing but another ideological separation between the exploited and subversives.[78]

Others point out that this critique glosses over the fact that members of the working class take part in Black Blocs, as suggested by numerous Black Bloc communiqués and declarations published over the years. In particular, the communiqué "Who Is the Black Bloc? Where Is the Black Bloc?", released in 2010 by the Italian Autonomous University Collective in the wake of some student protest actions, asked:

> Do you want to see the faces behind the scarves, helmets, balaclavas? They are the same faces that pay your rent for derelict houses; the faces you look at when asking to sign work contracts of 500 euros a month ... They are the faces that submit dissertation proposals and are obliged to reference your boring texts ... they make your cappuccino with froth ... They are the ones whose lifeblood is being sapped by financial insecurity, whose lives are shit, and they are tired of putting up with it.[79]

This quotation offers a portrait of Black Blockers as respectable citizens, as good workers and diligent students. It also indicates that their revolt is legitimate because they are dominated by an unfair and inegalitarian system.

Furthermore, many statements made by wage earners who are not Black Blockers convey their sympathy for direct action in general and for anarchists using the Black Bloc tactic in particular. To quote a worker who was present at the Battle of Seattle:

> Isn't there anyone who will defend the anarchists? ... These young men and women, aren't they our comrades rather than saboteurs of our movement? Shouldn't we, on the contrary, thank these

revolutionary spirits for expressing a righteous anger and refusing a globalized social order based on greed, systemic violence, and the oppression of the majority? ... In response to police brutality, the nonviolence advocated by most organizations has proved totally inadequate ... Finally, demonstrations were not the exclusive property of the pacifists, ecologists, unions, and religious groups *any more* than they were the anarchists'. No one has a monopoly on the streets ... And yet, as a man of colour and a member of the working class, I consider it an honour to have shared the company, during the dark days of Seattle, of these young and valiant idealistic rebels."[80]

For another observer,

The true heroes of the Battle in Seattle [were] the street warriors, the Ruckus Society, the Anarchists, Earth Firsters, the Direct Action Media Network (DAMN), radical labor militants such as the folks at Jobs With Justice, hundreds of Longshoremen, Steelworkers Electrical Workers and Teamsters who disgustedly abandoned the respectable, police sanctioned official AFL-CIO parade and joined the street warriors at the barricades in downtown ... A few rebellious steelworkers, longshoremen, electrical workers and teamsters did disobey their leaders, push into downtown and join the battle. The main march withdrew in respectable good order and dispersed peacefully to their hotels ... Fortunately the street warriors won.[81]

At the demonstrations against the Summit of the Americas in Quebec City in April 2001, many individuals left the Peoples' March, organized and supervised by reformist institutions, at the invitation of activists encouraging them to join the crowd that was defying the police. The Peoples' March, some 60,000 strong, was supervised by the Fédération des travailleurs et travailleuses du Québec (FTQ: Quebec Federation of Labour) corps of marshals and confined to the *basse-ville* (lower town), even though the official Summit was taking place in the *haute-ville* (upper town). People waiting for the march to get under way needed only look up and see the *haute-ville* swathed in thick clouds of tear gas in order to realize how nasty the situation must be for the protesters up there. As planned by the organizers, the People's March turned its back on the dramatic events, moving farther away from the *haute-ville* and deeper into a residential neighbourhood, eventually ending up in a vacant lot several kilometres from the confrontation and the official Summit.

But not all union members agreed with the position of the labour bureaucracy, which tried to control labour's role at the protest. For example, members of local 3903 of the Canadian Union of Public Employees (CUPE), representing teaching assistants, graduate assistants, and contract faculty at York University (Toronto), along with York undergraduate students, had hired school buses to travel to Quebec City. Most of the members of CUPE 3903 who came were organized in affinity groups and had taken direct action training, legal training, and safety training. Some of these affinity groups had prepared for direct action with locks, chains, and other hardware, and at least one group was effectively a Black Bloc. Others joined Black Bloc actions when they got there. CUPE's national leaders had stated in an official press release that they would support civil disobedience and would be "on the front line," though it is doubtful they had Black Bloc-style direct action in mind.[82]

Then, as one CUPE member recalls,

during the People's March on the second day of the protests, many of the rank and file were furious that labour officials were leading them away to the middle of nowhere ... We had planned to head up the hill ourselves and to try to encourage others to follow. All of the CUPE Ontario leadership went up the hill with us ... There may have been CUPE leaders from other provinces there as well. People from other unions went up that hill too (lots of members of the Canadian Auto Workers) and were gassed and abused by the cops. At the top of the hill we saw Black Blocs and union members (mostly big burly Canadian Auto Workers) working together with a grappling hook and a rope, trying to pull the fence down. They faced gas and water cannon ... After the Summit, at the CUPE

Ontario convention in Ottawa in June, CUPE national President Judy Darcy gave a passionate speech to the members in which she said that labour would not abandon the young people at the wall again, that every local would get direct action training, and that every local would be sent gas masks ... So, all this is to say that the division between labour and Black Blocs is not so clear.[83]

In the Quebec City neighbourhoods where the confrontations took place, a number of residents supported the activists by giving them water, cheering them on from their balconies, or opening their doors when they needed to take refuge. Similar scenes were witnessed in Genoa in 2001.

Another example is provided by Mohammed Chikkaoui, a spokesperson for Oxfam-Québec, who commented on the four windows broken in downtown Montreal during an anti-WTO demonstration in 2003: "When we see the ongoing obstruction and incoherence in international institutions, and we watch people, young people in the street with expectations for the future who see that the future has nothing good in store for them ... If I were their age, I might have done the same thing."[84]

Addressing several hundred people at Vittorio Square in Turin, Italy, on July 8, 2011, Alberto Perino, for twenty years the spokesperson of the No TAV movement in Val di Susa, declared, "Siamo tutti Black Bloc" (We are all Black Blocs), and was cheered by the crowd.[85] The slogan *Siamo tutti Black Bloc* even appears on T-shirts sold in that region to support the No TAV movement.

At an October 2013 assembly, in response to a clash between police and demonstrators, members of Brazil's State Union of Education Professionals (SEPE) expressed unconditional support for the Black Blocs. Many teachers said that they had been protected by the Bloc and a general coordinator for SEPE stated that "the Black Blocs are always welcome" in their demonstrations.

In sum, there is no truth to claims that the operations of the Black Blocs necessarily widen the gap between anarchism and "ordinary" working-class citizens.

This Is What Democracy Looks Like!

Representatives of progressive movements and organizations accuse the Black Blocs and their allies of not respecting the "democratic" process. This was the central argument advanced by Michael Albert after the events in Seattle in 1999 in his article, "On trashing and movement building."

The assumptions underlying these criticisms of Black Blocs stem from a homogeneous vision whereby a social movement should be unified and march in a single direction determined by enlightened leaders who are comfortably installed at the head of organizations that are supposedly "responsible," "democratic," and "representative" of "civil society" as a whole. But the Black Blocs are based on a very different political rationale. They have no "respectable" personalities ensuring that their discourse is taken up by the mainstream media, nor do they wish to be financed by the state and invited to discussions with members of the G20, the G8, or the participants in the World Economic Forum in Davos. Black Bloc activists declare instead: "We are not looking for a seat in the discussions among the masters of the world; we want the masters of the world to no longer exist."[86]

Clearly, the frictions that have developed within the alter-globalization and anti-austerity social movements reflect two different conceptions of democracy. The self-proclaimed "representatives" of the movement defend representative democracy. For a community—be it a nation or a social movement—to be "represented," it must be perceived as homogeneous and as able to express itself through a single voice (that of its representatives). This approach is exemplified by Patti Goldman, managing attorney with Earthjustice, founded as the Sierra Club Legal Defense Fund in Seattle in 1971, who stated in 1999, in Seattle:

> We condemn the violence. We are a legal institution that works through the law to protect the environment. There are valid arguments to be made to the WTO and the Clinton administration about a critical need for fundamental reform of trade rules to protect our

> health and our environment. Violence only obscures our message.
> A handful of anarchists should not drown out the message of thou-
> sands of peaceful marchers.[87]

What her words actually show, however, is that there is no unified movement; instead there are power relationships, in the course
of which social movement elites try to distance themselves from the
"anarchists," to shut them out without the slightest acknowledgment
that the anarchists' message may somehow be relevant.

Regarding the "diversity of tactics," Susan George asserts that this
approach cannot work because "there will be no *unity* in the demonstration and *no clear message* for the outside world."[88] The implication
is that George can speak for the entire movement, from which she has
excluded the deviant elements. As for the Black Blocs, she dismisses
them as "a handful of individuals who, in effect, have nothing to propose."[89] In reference to the anti-G8 Summit demonstrations in Évian,
she adds that the "vandals" belonged to a "minority subculture ... the
'black leather heavy metal spike hair' unwashed of Zurich, whose sole
aim in life is apparently to smash things. Only a qualified psycholo-
gist or anthropologist could say if they have any interest whatsoever
in politics."[90]

The Black Blocs and their allies are described as products of cultural deviance combined with psychological pathology. In this way,
they serve as foils for the leaders of institutionalized groups, who, by
dissociating themselves from the "vandals," hope to project a calm,
respectable, and homogeneous image of a movement that can speak
with one voice, that of its elite.

By contrast, anarchists and the majority of those who participate
in Black Blocs view a social movement as something heterogeneous,
as a movement of movements, and hold that the multitude cannot be
"represented" without its will being oversimplified by the representing
elite. In other words, that the delegation of authority undermines the
principles of equality and freedom, because representatives invariably
develop personal interests at odds with the "common good" of the community they claim to represent. The members of the Black Blocs favour

pluralism and autonomy of choice, whereas progressive elites seek to discipline "their" demonstrations and publicly condemn the Black Blocs' actions. Feeling that they have been betrayed, Black Blockers sometimes intentionally disrupt the speeches of high-profile leaders of the movement. An incident like this happened in Nice in December 2000, in the prelude to the EU Summit there. A French activist recounts what happened at gatherings held prior to the demonstrations:

> There were about 200 of us sleeping in the basement of a carpark. I experienced the horror familiar to itinerants who sleep on cardboard, with the cold burning your back. I was there because we could talk about violence. We had excluded ourselves from the gymnasium, where people like Susan George and Alain Krivine[91] were speaking. That was the first time I realized you could disrupt people. Usually, they are the ones—on the issue of "illegal immigrants" or other topics—who cut us out, who co-opt us, who appropriate movements by sending their youths to our general meetings, but this time we shouted insults at them and hooted them down.[92]

Here, the "representatives" of the movement were being faulted for denying its diversity and for refusing to take its radical, anti-authoritarian components seriously.

Yet at the same time, and even worse, the elite endeavours to link up with popular movements and co-opt their militant energy for its own benefit or for the benefit of institutionalized organizations. The musician Midge Ure, organizer of the Scottish Live8 in 2005, was asked by journalists whether he feared that the anarchists would co-opt Live8 (a series of music events with a lineup of stars demanding debt cancellation for the poorest nations). He replied that in fact, he was turning the anarchists' event to his advantage.[93] Yet after the demonstrations, he told the anarchists to "go home."[94]

Those who join Black Blocs do not view their political commitment solely in relation to, for example, an alter-globalization movement with a single, clear, and specific goal. This is mainly because that movement is composed primarily of institutionalized progressive organizations. In this connection, a member of an affinity group allied with the Black Blocs explains: "We are anticapitalists first, before being opponents of globalization; we are against globalization because we are anticapitalists."[95] This is why the Black Blocs often criticize the progressive elite for being wishy-washy. So each side accuses the other of sapping the movement's effectiveness and credibility.

The elites of reformist organizations constantly chastise "young rioters" and "anarchists" in the belief that this will make the reformist leaders worthy of the state's and the media's attention. The mainstream political arena is under the sway of a full-fledged normalizing apparatus, which consists of government policies, official communication channels, grants, criteria for inclusion (or exclusion), and so on. The dependence of progressive political actors on this apparatus encourages them to dissociate themselves from groups that might tarnish their respectability. Indeed, the financial and political fate of the spokespersons of various institutions often depends as much on government subsidies as on the success or failure of their actions.

Representatives of the state have openly asked the spokespersons of reformist organizations to publicly dissociate themselves from the "rioters." In the wake of the disturbances related to the G8 Summit in Genoa, in 2001, Guy Verhofstadt, Prime Minister of Belgium and President of the EU, demanded: "I want to hear the representatives of all democratic movements and parties, throughout the world, to distance themselves from the rioters."[96] This injunction was taken up by commentators like Dominique Von Burg, editor-in-chief of *La Tribune de Genève,* in his front-page analysis of the demonstrations against the G8 Summit in Évian in June 2003. He depicted the "vandals" as no more than "a handful of imbeciles": "A few hundred rioters ... managed to steal the show from a peaceful and important protest ... As they did during the demonstration, the opposition forces *must resolutely reject* all those whose arguments add up to crowbars and Molotov cocktails."[97]

The progressive elite appears to be amenable to calls like these. When he was in charge of international relations for ATTAC, Christophe Aguiton, though more radical than Susan George and ready to denounce police violence, declared that the Social Forum organized by reformist groups and associations in Genoa in 2001 "was *legitimized, in Italy and far beyond, by its ability to differentiate itself from the acts of violence* committed by certain groups of demonstrators."[98] The same point was made during the Summit of the Americas in Quebec City by Françoise David, spokesperson for the Peoples' Summit (subsidized by the governments of Canada and Quebec), who said "no to the violence," which according to her had been orchestrated by "a very small group" of vandals.[99] Finally, here was Bob Geldof's response, as spokesperson for the Live8 campaign, to the "violent" activists protesting the G8 Summit in Scotland in 2005: "You're a bunch of losers."[100]

The "Peace-Police"

In return for publicly denouncing the Black Blocs, the spokespersons of the progressive movement hope to be rewarded politically by the authorities. Specifically, they hope to be recognized as legitimate players and to receive invitations to discuss, and perhaps negotiate, with people in high places.[101] The reformists' desire to project a respectable image of themselves leads to the self-disciplining of street demonstrations. Of course, implicit even in peaceful demonstrations is the idea that a civil war or a revolution is possible. The French philosopher Yves Michaud observes: "In democratic countries, the mass demonstration is a ritualized form of confrontation. The adversaries show their numbers without the intention of using force but letting it be inferred that they could."[102] Reformist leaders who are concerned about their public image clearly intend that this potential clash be forever deferred.[103]

The question arises, however: What political relationship is being established when the progressive elite asks the authorities for permission to demonstrate, discusses the route of the march with them, and has the protesters supervised by a corps of marshals? The political scientist Olivier Fillieule refers to a "spirit of complicity"[104] between organizers and the police. Isabelle Sommier, also a political scientist, notes that "the requirements of internal order of a march" organized by the major militant institutions coincide with "the requirements of public order," because "both [are] threatened by 'uncontrollable' 'disruptive elements,' or 'vandals' of one sort or another."[105]

This being so, politicians and progressive spokespersons are on exactly the same page. "We firmly condemn this type of violent action, which is totally foreign to the alterglobalization movement," said Juan Tortosa, one of the co-ordinators of the Geneva-based Forum social lémanique, in response to actions carried out during the G8 Summit in Évian. In Genoa, José Bové, a member of the Confédération paysanne and undoubtedly the most renowned spokesperson for the alter-globalization movement in France, declared that "today, over 200,000 people have assembled here, refusing the rationale of the G8, the rationale of globalization, despite police provocations and despite the attempts at destabilization of a certain number of uncontrolled groups." The gist of these remarks, made on the public network France 2 on July 21, 2001, was reiterated the same day on TF1, where Bové again referred to "uncontrolled groups." Uncontrolled? By whom? The police? Or movement organizers and spokespersons such as Bové himself? A moot point. What is clear in all of this, however, is the idea that everything would be fine if all the demonstrators behaved in a "controlled" manner. As Christophe Aguiton of ATTAC bluntly stated: "It would be better if we could control everything."[106] Susan George, meanwhile, has declared it necessary "to impose overall non-violence in our ranks" in order to achieve "disciplined activism."[107]

For those who present themselves as the movement's spokespersons, what is at stake is controlling the rank and file, even to the point of acting as police auxiliaries. Hence, the protesting institutions' deployment of marshals in Seattle, Quebec City, Annemasse, Toronto, and elsewhere.

Following the 2010 G20 Summit in Toronto, Sid Ryan, president of the Ontario Federation of Labour, who had clearly changed his tune since marching up the hill with CUPE members in Quebec City in 2001, wrote a letter to the editor of the *Toronto Star* denouncing the "cowardly actions" of the "hooligans." Concerning the large People First demonstration organized by labour unions and civil society organizations, Ryan stated:

> The rally organizers, including the Ontario Federation of Labour, worked diligently to ensure that our democratic right to lawful assembly would be respected ... To this end, we liaised with the Toronto Police and cooperated at every turn. On the day, hundreds of volunteer marshals facilitated what was an extraordinarily successful event, given the tension that had pervaded the city in the days before.[108]

In his view, the People First protest "told world leaders—including our own Prime Minister Stephen Harper—to put the needs of human beings and the environment ahead of all other considerations as they deliberated over the weekend."

Chris Samuel examined the "distinction between People First and Get Off the Fence" at the Toronto G20 protests. Get Off the Fence was a demonstration called by the Community Solidarity network in which a Black Bloc took part. Samuel concluded that "by demonstrating that People First was not Black Bloc, People First organizers accumulated symbolic capital at Black Bloc's expense ... They used their institutional stability to maintain relations with police and thereby portray those relations as supporting legitimate protest."[109] But Samuel also noted that while this approach certainly harmed the Black Bloc's public image, it did not strengthen the impact of the People First demonstration on the G20 Summit discussions in particular or on global capitalism in general. As a rule, the political and financial elites that run the G20 show little interest in any demonstration that does not represent an actual threat to social stability.

A few progressive personalities have gone so far as to suggest that the police should move quickly to arrest members of the Black Blocs. For example, Judy Rebick, a progressive feminist intellectual in Canada, criticized the Black Blocs after the demonstrations and mass arrests during the Toronto G20. A few months earlier she had commented on the Black Bloc's action during the demonstrations against the Olympic Games in Vancouver: "If diversity of tactics means that people who aim to commit vandalism and sometimes violence can come into the middle of a demonstration with black face masks and break up whatever takes their fancy when the vast majority of people involved don't want them to, then I draw a line."[110] With regard to Toronto, given that the Black Bloc withdrew from the mass demonstration and dashed away in the opposite direction, one might have expected Judy Rebick to be satisfied. Instead she wrote,

> I believe the cops could have arrested the Black Bloc right at the beginning of the action but they abandoned their police cars and allowed them to burn ... I disagree with torching police cars and breaking windows and I have been debating these tactics for decades with people who think they accomplish something. But the bigger question here is why the police let it happen and make no mistake the police did let it happen. Why did the police let the city get out of control? ... It is the police that bear the responsibility for what happened last night. They were responsible for keeping the peace and they failed to do it.[111]

This statement, which is ambiguous to say the least, suggests that Rebick would have preferred to see the police arrest members of the Black Bloc.

About ten years earlier, Lori Wallach, an American lobbyist and director of Global Trade Watch, which is affiliated with Ralph Nader's Public Citizen organization, told an interviewer that on November 29, 1999, the day before the direct actions in Seattle, "anarchists" had wanted to break windows during an event where José Bové was distributing Roquefort cheese in front of a McDonald's:

> Our people actually picked up the anarchists. Because we had with us steelworkers and longshoremen who, by sheer bulk, were three or four times larger. So we had them literally just sort of, a teamster on either side, just pick up an anarchist. We'd walk him over to the cops and say this boy just broke a window. He doesn't belong to us. We hate the WTO, so does he, maybe, but we don't break things. Please arrest him. And the cops wouldn't arrest anyone.[112]

The next day, Medea Benjamin, who heads Global Exchange, based in San Francisco, and who campaigns against the sweatshops that supply Nike, intervened to protect the windows of Nike, McDonald's, and Gap against the "vandals." She told the *New York Times* that she had wondered, "Where are the police? These anarchists should have been arrested."[113] It is more than a little troubling to see reformist spokespersons sharing this desire for discipline with politicians, police officers, and even the heads of multinationals. In September 1998, 450 of the latter signed the Geneva Business Declaration, which contained a statement that José Bové, Susan George, and other reformist leaders would not dispute: "Business is accustomed to working with trade unions, consumer organizations and other representative groups that are responsible, credible, transparent and accountable and consequently command respect. What we question is the proliferation of activist groups that do not accept these self-disciplinary criteria."[114]

In her study of the demonstrations against the Summit of the Americas, Isabelle Saint-Armand has noted that the "cartoon portrait of the vandal, poles apart from that of the peaceful protester, helps to split the demonstrators on grounds of morality and legitimacy."[115] Moreover, politicians, police officials, and representatives of the state know how to express their gratitude to the leaders of progressive organizations for effectively supervising demonstrations and observing previously negotiated agreements on meeting points, starting times, and routes. Concerning the mass demonstration against the G8 Summit in Évian in June 2003, Laurent Moutinot, president of the Swiss State Council, offered bouquets as well as brickbats: "With regard to the demonstration itself, it is difficult to find fault with the organizers . . . They adhered to the agreements arrived at with them. But they were confronted with people who use this type of event for their own purposes. It is a phenomenon akin to the hooligans."[116]

Christophe Aguiton, who was in charge of liaising between a number of militant organizations and the police during the Évian Summit, received a gift of two beautiful knives from the chief of police for having played by the rules established largely by the authorities. This little ceremony was broadcast by the media, of course, which gave the chief of police the chance to project a friendly image of the police in front of the TV cameras.

Clearly, out of an unhealthy desire to co-operate with the authorities and to be seen as reasonable and responsible, some radical and dynamic activists find themselves playing walk-on roles in a show that benefits the very authorities they claim to be opposing. In this connection, the French militant Patrice Spadoni, a former postal worker and the organizer of the Marches Against Unemployment in Europe, explains, "What frightens the powers that be is the conjunction of radicalism and mass movements." He adds: "The powers that be seek to divide the protest movement, which has more and more support. On one hand, they want to criminalize the combative wing of the social movements. On the other, they try to integrate the most moderate wing."[117]

Politicians and police officials appreciate it when protesters discipline themselves and organize their own parapolice corps in the shape of marshals. The *Marche des peuples* (Peoples' March), held during the 2001 Summit of the Americas in Quebec City, is exemplary in this regard. Having been informed that Black Blocs intended to join the demonstration, one of the FTQ's union marshals declared on that organization's communications network: "Okay, I'll send you some muscle! We'll deal with them in short order."[118] This soon gave rise to a series of congratulatory remarks. After the Marche des peuples, Canadian prime minister Jean Chrétien said: "I'd like to take this opportunity to thank the QFL, which had its own security guards."[119] The comments made by Bernard Landry, then Premier of Quebec, display the same political bias:

> The demonstration of the Peoples' Summit was exceptionally peaceful and exemplary. I am told the labour unions' corps of marshals fulfilled their roles very well. We know that, traditionally, the Quebec Federation of Labour and the Confederation of National Trade Unions are able to ensure order in demonstrations. They did this successfully, but it should be recalled that demonstrations can be infiltrated by vandals whose behaviour is antidemocratic and antisocial, who are not angels and deserve none of our sympathy.[120]

"It was organized by serious-minded people. It was impeccable," was how Robert Poeti, spokesman for the police, expressed himself.[121] But a demonstrator who had taken part in the very calm *Marche des peuples* vented his disappointment in an open letter. He was less enthusiastic about the organizers, who he felt had fooled him: "I played the game by participating in the peaceful demonstration ... I decided to put my trust in nonviolent protest and to continue along the planned route, even though it led straight to a suburban wasteland ... How naïve I was! We played the game, but we were the only ones. The media hardly mentioned our march."[122]

CONCLUSION

POLICE REPRESSION AND POLITICAL PROFILING

One consequence of the Black Blocs' popularity is that they no longer have the advantage of surprise; this has made them more vulnerable to repression, surveillance, and police infiltration. For example, the report produced by the Toronto Police Service after the G20 Summit of 2010 contains excerpts from its operational logbook with almost minute-by-minute updates sent to the command centre. The document brings to light the police's apparent obsession with the Black Blocs, to the point that, even as the events of the Summit unfolded, the police circulated often useless and sometimes preposterous "information" on anything possibly resembling a Black Bloc. During the peaceful march of June 25, the police officers keeping watch informed their commanders that some 30 Black Blockers were chanting "Bomb the RBC" (Royal Bank of Canada) and that the odour of something burning a few minutes later could mean that Molotov cocktails were being prepared. A team of bomb disposal experts was deployed when the members of the Black Bloc seemed to be readying a makeshift bomb in front of police headquarters. The police observers also reported seeing "more Black Bloc members ... masking up and putting on goggles. A number of them also began to mix unknown liquids or chemicals in plastic bags and glass jars."[1] Several hours after the start of the demonstration, "Black Bloc members" were seen once again "mixing unknown liquids together out front of the Sick Kids Hospital,"[2] and a little later, "Black Bloc members were observed urinating into pop bottles in apparent preparation for something."[3] Actually, this demonstration ended just as it had begun, that is, altogether peacefully, with no Black Blocs carrying out any direct actions.

The police's obsession with the Black Blocs makes it risky to undertake certain actions, especially in small-scale demonstrations but even at mass rallies. As Black Blocs are highly visible, the police can easily slip into a crowd and apprehend members of the group. That is what happened in Montreal (2012) during a march against increased rates for public services, in New York (January–February 2002), during the World Economic Forum, and in Ottawa (November 2001) during demonstrations against the IMF, World Bank, and G20.[4]

Black Blocs are particularly vulnerable to police infiltration and *agents provocateurs*. The wearing of masks actually facilitates infiltration, and one can easily imagine police officers in disguise circulating in small groups and arresting unsuspecting protesters. Furthermore, *agents provocateurs* can commit illegal and possibly violent acts to manipulate genuine demonstrators as well as the media and thereby justify more aggressive police interventions.

These concerns are expressed after almost every major mobilization involving confrontations and repression, by spokespersons of political organizations as well as by rank-and-file activists. Their typical contention is that police agents were part of the Black Bloc and had manipulated it. Often, though, the evidence supporting these claims is a few pictures shown out of context—for instance, of a Black Blocker who seems to be talking to riot police—with no indication of what is actually being said or of what happened before or after the shot was taken, or of what was going on beyond the frame.

At the 2001 G8 Summit in Genoa, various rumours circulated to the effect that the Black Bloc had colluded with the police or that the Italian authorities had let hundreds of neo-Nazis come to Genoa to foment trouble disguised as Black Blockers in order to discredit the movement and justify repression.[5] Susan George was particularly energetic in relaying these stories, declaring that "the Black Blocs are *very*

The security fence after it was torn down by Blocs and other protesters at the Summit of the Americas in Quebec City, April 2001.

often infiltrated by the police and Nazi elements."[6] In his recent book about the Black Blocs, the Italian journalist Franco Fracassi tries to demonstrate on the basis of interviews with retired police officers that the Black Blocs have been infiltrated and controlled by secret service agents, unbeknownst to other police forces. He goes so far as to claim that the Black Blocs are financed by private foundations and multinational corporations to create chaos and discredit the demands of progressive forces.

Another way to "prove" that police manipulation is at work is to point out that the police are always well informed about the Black Blocs but do nothing to arrest them before a demonstration or to limit their actions while it is ongoing. In June 2010, after the G20 protests in Toronto, Murray Dobbin, a senior editor of the progressive webzine *rabble* (launched in 2001, just days before the Summit of the Americas in Quebec City), explained that the police forces know exactly what they are doing ... the obvious fact is that they were always in control. This was a very strategic operation from beginning to end. The decision to allow the Black Bloc to do its destructive work without any intervention at all was strategic as the police and their political masters knew the media would play their pre-assigned reactionary role and focus on the destruction of property. The mass arrest of 900 people [in the end, more than 1,100] was a message to those willing to take a stand: you could be next, and a criminal record is no laughing matter. There is no question that amongst the mob of window-breakers and car-burners were a significant number of *agents provocateurs* ... Perhaps next time the real social activists should swarm these people and stop them if the police refuse. They are the enemies of social change—we should treat all of them as *agents provocateurs* and plan to deal with them accordingly. In the process we might catch a few more cops in the act.[7]

Dobbin is suggesting here that demonstrators should physically attack Black Bloc activists, effectively serving as a kind of "peace police." He is also claiming that the police are "always in control"—except, no doubt, when people demonstrate peacefully and without disrupting the social order.

Regarding the 2001 demonstrations against the G8, Fracassi referred in his book to a document filed in the Genoese courts titled "Informazioni sul fronte della protesta anti G8" (Information on the anti-G8 protest front), which indicated very precisely the number of anarchists expected from all over Europe as well as the number of activists representing a threat in Italy: in Aosta, ten Black Blockers and forty Pink Bloc members; in Perugia, five Black Blockers; in Vibo Valentia, three Pink Bloc members and one Blue Bloc (I have no idea what a "Blue" Bloc might be!).[8] Fracassi also reported that the Italian police were aware of 1,891 activists participating in Black Blocs in Italy.[9] He wondered why they were not arrested, and concluded that their remaining free was further "proof" of police manipulation.

All of this is somewhat ridiculous. Besides, preventive arrests of activists pose an obvious threat to political freedom. There is little doubt that the authorities collect fairly sound data on protest groups and use that information when conducting operations such as crowd control. None of which can ensure that everyone who represents a public security risk will be either prevented from acting or caught in the act. Even so, mass demonstrations are typically subjected to surveillance, infiltration, preventive arrests, and border stoppages, as was the case in Genoa in 2001, when the Italian authorities stopped trains and turned away ferry boats. In 2011, at the G20 Summit in Cannes, the police tried to intercept "troublemakers" at the French–Italian border,[10] and a number of Spanish activists were indeed arrested on the morning of the demonstrations.[11] The London police made 57 arrests in June 2013 at the gathering point for the Carnival Against Capitalism, part of the protests against the G8 Summit in Ireland. According to the police, the arrests were justified by "intelligence that individuals at the address were in possession of weapons and were intent on causing criminal damage and engaging in violent disorder."[12] The fact is that the police regularly carry out preventive arrests just before major mobilizations, apparently with the aim of destabilizing militant networks and presenting the public with an image of efficiency.

After the 2010 G20 Summit in Toronto the police distributed dozens of photos, and individuals suspected of having committed an offence were arrested in the ensuing weeks, not just in Toronto but also in Vancouver and the United States. In sum, security services and police forces are very powerful, endowed with sophisticated surveillance resources, and well equipped for encounters with large crowds and to prosecute suspects.

But this does not mean the police are omniscient, omnipotent, and immune to incompetence. At the October 2011 demonstration of the Occupy Movement in Rome, police officers were deployed in small groups to protect government buildings. Demonstrators later attested they had seen these units doing nothing while the demonstration grew increasingly rowdy, because they had been ordered to stand fast in front of the buildings. The next day, the front-page headlines of *La Repubblica* summed up the results of that decision: "The black bloc devastates Rome. Seventy wounded, among them ten officers. Carabinieri's van burned. Police handling of violent protesters criticized."[13]

At the 2010 G20 Summit in Toronto, many were surprised that the rows of anti-riot police blocking the streets that led to the security fence remained immobile while the Black Bloc ran right under their noses in the opposite direction, smashing windows along the way. And why was it that the anti-riot units brought in by van never caught and neutralized the Black Bloc? The many reports produced after the Summit by the police, the Ontario ombudsman, and the Independent Police Review make it clear that the police thought the Black Bloc's intention was to break through the police lines to reach the security fence.[14] Thus, the anti-riot squads had received orders not to budge, not to be distracted, and to stay put and block the streets leading to the fence. Indeed, the police thought it possible that the Black Bloc would smash windows as a diversion to draw the anti-riot squads away from the security fence. As for the vans transporting mobile police units, many found themselves simply stuck in traffic. Others were driven by civilians who were not authorized to run red lights, or by officers from outside Toronto whose knowledge of the city was so poor they were obliged to stop to buy city maps at subway stations so that they could make sense of their orders. The upshot was that, despite the hundreds of millions spent on security, the deployment of thousands of police officers, and the months spent on police infiltration that resulted in the "preventive" arrest of 17 anarchists before the demonstration, the Black Bloc enjoyed about 45 minutes of freedom to smash dozens of windows in downtown Toronto. To quote the report of the Office of the Independent Police Review Director (OIPRD): "There was clearly a rising level of frustration among both the officers on the ground and the commanding officers ... about the lack of control that the police appeared to have over the protest on the streets and their inability to stop the Black Bloc vandals."

The police chief called an emergency meeting, and when the change of shift took place at the command post, the new officer in charge—according to a police officer's testimony—"wanted the streets that had been made unsafe by the terrorists that were attacking our city to be made safe again by restoring order." This meant "mass arrests." The OIPRD report notes that the commanders were "scrambling to react" and that the "result was an overreaction."[15] The police began to charge the crowd, making hundreds of arrests, yet by then the Black Bloc had vanished, leaving behind piles of black clothing in public parks. By the time the Summit ended, more than a thousand arrests had been made, 96 percent of which ultimately would not lead to charges, let alone trials.[16]

Police Infiltration

Setting aside the paranoiacs and supporters of conspiracy theories who believe the police actually *can* control everyone everywhere at all times, there is no question that police infiltrate and manipulate activist groups, and, moreover, that they use activists as police informers. In the United Kingdom, a number of female activists took legal action after a dozen police agents had infiltrated their network and had intimate relations with them, sometimes over many years. In one case this had led to the birth of a child. Adding to the absurdity, one of the unmasked agents sued the police for psychological injury: "My superiors knew who I was sleeping with but chose to turn a blind eye because I was getting such valuable information. They did nothing to prevent me falling in love."[17] This police spy, Mark Kennedy, operated for about seven years in a dozen European countries, infiltrating far left networks and providing information on anarchist groups as well as on "an anti-fascist group whose main objective was to disrupt the activities of the extreme far right wing groups and political parties."[18] It appears that some of the intelligence he gathered helped indict a number of activists.[19]

Several months before the mobilizations against the Toronto G20 Summit, the police planted undercover agents, especially in the Southern Ontario Anarchist Network (SOAR). One of the agents was so successful she became the roommate of one of the militant women and was able to record meetings of the group. She would eventually serve as the main witness against the 17 anarchists arrested for a conspiracy of which they were said to be the "ring leaders." And in April 2001,

48 hours before the official opening of the Summit of the Americas in Quebec City, members of an affinity group called Germinal were intercepted in a private car on the highway between Montreal and Quebec. The police found defensive and offensive gear in the vehicle, and the militants spent several weeks behind bars. By what miracle were the police able to spot these militants in an ordinary automobile among so many others on the highway? Simple: two RCMP agents— who later would testify at the trial—had infiltrated the group several months earlier. The operation was extremely useful for the authorities, for it allowed them to neutralize a handful of activists and exhibit the police's "spoils of war" to the media on the eve of the Quebec Summit. To anyone paying attention, this amounted to a declaration that police efficiency was at its peak. Some have contended that this is a common police strategy in the run-up to summits.

Infiltration also occurs when protests are in progress, with plain-clothes police officers deployed directly among the protesters. During the G8 Summit in Évian in 2003, a group of officers formed what appeared to be a Black Bloc, marched into the convergence centre located in the self-managed cultural centre l'Usine (the Factory) in the heart of Geneva, and immediately carried out a series of forceful arrests. Images of the intervention were widely distributed through the mass and alternative media, and the Swiss police publicly claimed responsibility for the operation.[20] In 2008, during the mobilizations against the Security and Prosperity Partnership of North America Summit in Montebello, Quebec, three agents of the Sûreté du Québec, as part of an operation ironically named "Flagrant Délit" (i.e., caught red-handed), disguised themselves in black in order to infiltrate the Black Bloc. One of them held a rock in his hand as he moved about. Sensing the subterfuge, the Black Blockers held them at bay; soon afterwards, they were literally unmasked by trade unionists. To extricate themselves from their predicament, the three agents slipped behind a police line and lay down on the ground as if under arrest. But video recordings later showed that the arresting officers and those being arrested were wearing identical boots. The SQ eventually admitted that the three individuals were police officers. Moreover, a request under the Access to Information Act revealed that the special undercover unit Flagrant Délit had 35 officers mobilized solely for the Montebello Summit (even though the protest of about 1,200 people lasted no more than a few hours).[21]

Although the Black Blocs remain vulnerable to infiltration, working through affinity groups somewhat reduces the risk of manipulation because, in principle, the members of such groups know one another well. Moreover, a police infiltrator could never climb to the top of the organization and set a trap for the militants, quite simply because "top" positions do not exist, nor do "leaders." Thus, despite the arrest of the supposed "ring leaders" in Toronto, in 2010, on the morning before the mass demonstration the Black Bloc was able to smash dozens of windows. It does not take a "leader" to start a riot.

A participant in Black Blocs in Quebec said that "it would be naïve not to grant that [infiltration] is possible. But the Black Blocs say it's the other way around: it's the moderate groups that are infiltrated and manipulated by the police."[22] Indeed, it is more than likely that reformist organizations are also infiltrated by the police, and in any case the leaders of such organizations (including unions) are usually glad to help the police, to heed police concerns while planning mobilizations, and to provide their own marshals as police auxiliaries. Yet leaders of institutionalized or parliamentary progressive groups often assert that police manipulate Black Blocs. Such groups find it advantageous to discredit anarchists. To quote Victor Serge, an anarchist and later a communist in the early twentieth century,

> against their enemies the anarchists—those perennial gadflies— social-democratic politicians [have often used] the vilest, deadliest weapon: slander … It is a tradition and a tactic … Let any anarchist, pushed to the brink by the daily vexations of honest folk, commit an act, and you will hear screams of "provocateur!" You are forbidden to move on pain of being smeared. You are forbidden to rebel against the arbitrary on pain of being branded a stoolpigeon.[23]

Once rumours are spread and doubt is sown in people's minds, how is one to distinguish true from false?[24]

Political Profiling

The violence of the Black Blocs and their allies sets in motion an apparently simple mechanism: police repression and brutality.[25] It can surprise no one that, after windows have been smashed and project-iles hurled at citizens in uniform, they do not offer to settle the mat-ter by flipping a coin. After all, the protesters knowingly break the law and sometimes target the police themselves. And if anyone rejects dogmatic non-violence, surely it is the police. Black Blockers must ser-iously consider the consequences of their actions for other demonstra-tors, but it would be a mistake to hold them responsible for the choices made by the police.

The dynamic between activists and the police is actually quite complex, and police violence does not always arise in response to that of the protesters. In other words, the police do not need a Black Bloc's presence for an excuse to lash out at demonstrators; they sometimes willingly manhandle, injure, and arrest those who, objectively, do not represent a threat. Demonstrators' use of force may increase the risk of police brutality and arrests, but beyond that, the correlation is hard to find. The police have displayed a great deal of tolerance toward certain misdeeds, including the hurling of projectiles in their direction, while at other times they have assaulted and repressed altogether peace-ful protesters. During the Quebec student strike of 2012, some 3,500 people were arrested, many of them during mass kettlings of peace-ful demonstrations; yet there were also situations where the police allowed demonstrations to continue even when projectiles had been hurled at them.[26]

In other words, the police can always choose to intervene or not and, if they do, to use this or that particular weapon with more or less force. In Montreal on April 26, 2002, a demonstration some 500 strong against a preparatory meeting of G8 labour ministers never material-ized because the police kettled the crowd even before the march got under way, arresting everyone, protesters and bystanders alike. In Genoa in 2001, the police brutally kicked and clubbed a great many non-violent demonstrators, as confirmed by testimonies and televised

Police flee as their attempt to arrest May Day demonstrators is met with stones, Berlin, May 1, 1989.

images.[27] In Seattle, pictures taken by activists and the police clearly indicate that the Black Bloc's assaults on businesses and banks began hours *after* police officers had forcefully dispersed non-violent protesters who were blocking the streets and the entrances to the conference centre.[28] At the 1997 Asian Pacific Economic Community (APEC) Summit in Vancouver, activists were arrested for hanging signs saying "Free Speech" and "Democracy" on the security fence.[29]

The particular psychology of police officers may partly explain the repression and violence, but the police should not be censured on the grounds often invoked to condemn the Black Blocs—that is, of using violence merely for sadistic pleasure. Police violence can also be understood in social and political terms. The police, especially in North America, carry out "preventive" mass arrests to maintain their public image. Fearing that incidents of "vandalism" will earn them sharp criticism from the public, they opt for "prevention." Research by sociologists and political scientists has found that police officers resort to violence more readily if they know they are confronting political groups regarded as "deviant" or "marginal" by representatives of the state and political actors deemed respectable by the state.[30] This amounts to *political profiling*.[31] In a comparative study of over a thousand demonstrations held in Vancouver, Toronto, and Montreal, the sociologist Patrick Rafail observed that police cultures vary from one city to the next. He noted that mass arrests are more frequent in Montreal and that 22 percent of demonstrations in that city involved arrests, compared to 10 percent in Toronto and 4 percent in Vancouver.[32] He concluded that what the demonstrators actually do (or not) is not the primary factor in police brutality. Rather, in Vancouver, it is the association of a demonstration with counterculture groups, and in Toronto, it is the event's identification with radicalism. In Montreal, it is the particular theme of the demonstration that increases the risk of police brutality; the police there abhor protests against capitalism ... or police brutality.[33] In each of these cities, the main determinant of police brutality is who the protesters are in the eyes of the police, not the protesters' actions or lack thereof.

Over the years, intelligence agencies and the police, as well as some academics, have succeeded in publicly constructing the image of the "criminal anarchist" as a threat to public security or—worse—a proto-terrorist or even an actual terrorist.[34] In his study of police repression of the alter-globalization movement in Canada and the United States, Luis A. Fernandez has referred to this as the "violent anarchist frame," which is adopted by both the media and the police.[35] The Black Bloc plays a significant role in this connection, because it fully embodies the image of the violent and criminal anarchist. Regarding this threat, newspapers regularly reproduce rumours, for which the source is often the police themselves. In the winter of 2002, just before the World Economic Forum in New York, the *New York Daily News* announced that the police were worried about the possible presence of "Black Blocs." The same rumour was spread by the *Calgary Herald* a few weeks before the G8 Summit in Kananaskis in 2002: "A newly obtained report, prepared by the Canadian Security Intelligence

Service, says radical Black Block elements that disrupted previous international summits likely will organize for the conference."[36]

Occasionally the newspapers see red on their own, without any help from the police. For example, following the death of Margaret Thatcher, the *Mail Online* published an article under the sensational headline "Black Bloc: Name of the sinister group plotting to sabotage Baroness Thatcher's funeral with 're-enactment' of poll-tax riots."[37] As we have seen, the Black Bloc may constitute a threat to public order, but that threat is often overblown by the media and the authorities, and this has a direct impact on the extent of the repression.

In advance of the 2010 G8 summit in Huntsville, Ontario, scheduled just a few days before the G20 Summit in Toronto, the Joint Intelligence Group prepared a report (made available on the website of CBC/Radio-Canada) that identified among the various threats "criminal extremists motivated by a variety of radical ideologies," including "variants of anarchism, anarcho-syndicalism, nihilism, socialism and/ or communism." The report pointed out that "the existence of these ideologies and the grievances that emanate from them are not, in themselves, problematic" and that "differences in opinion are intrinsic to any democratic system. The core of the problem, however, is the evolution of these philosophical differences into the advocating of criminal activity ... Given the high profile of the political philosophy of anarchy within this milieu, it is instructive to note that anarchists pursue a destruction of law, order and government as a precursor to the imposition of anarchy."[38] This last comment suggests that anarchism directly threatens to destroy the state because this is what its political philosophy proposes, regardless of the actual weakness of anarchist networks, a weakness that in reality precludes the destruction of the state and "the imposition of anarchy."[39]

In their 2012 examination of the events of the Toronto G20 Summit, Jeffrey Monaghan and Kevin Walby proposed the concept of "threat amplification" to describe this process.[40] Working with some media and activists (the G20 Research Group), they used the Access to Information Act to obtain various documents concerning police preparations ahead of the G20 Summit, including notes for a three-hour training session titled "G20 Face to Face—Front Line Officer Training," which had been provided to police officers who were to be deployed in the streets. One section, titled "Protestors vs. Anarchists," distinguished between legal and legitimate demonstrators on one hand and criminal anarchists on the other. The training session referred explicitly to the Black Bloc, and the attendees were encouraged at the close of the session to "go home or to your work station and google Black Bloc, look at their behaviour, clothing, and listen to their reasons."[41] According to Monaghan and Walby, the surveillance and intelligence activities ahead of the events resulted in a "threat amplification," which then affected the practice of political profiling.[42] At the trial of a Toronto citizen who had been arrested during the demonstrations while he was on his way to a music show, the arresting sergeant testified that he had received training on the subject of the Black Bloc and felt that because the accused was dressed in black he fit the relevant description. This statement was corroborated by a detective who was called as a witness. For Monaghan and Walby, this is a typical example of the problematic effect of "threat amplification." The accused had been strip-searched and detained for two days before being released on $25,000 bail and placed under house arrest at the home of his father-in-law, who acted as his bondsman. It took more than a year from the time of his arrest for these conditions to be dropped.[43]

In tandem with police preparedness, the state sets up a repressive security system and an "anti-terrorist" apparatus; apparently this does not trouble the portion of the population that, due to the mendacious discourses issuing from various quarters, trembles at the mere thought of "young anarchist vandals" whose sole aim is to "trash everything." Even though the violence and destruction involved in anarchist and Black Bloc actions are relatively limited, the political authorities in the West have succeeded over time in propagating a figure of the anarchist as a veritable "interior enemy."[44] This serves to justify police operations designed to neutralize militants before they take any action, an objective achieved through "advanced identification" and a degree of criminalization incommensurate with the anarchists' actions.[45] In 2008 in France, an "anti-terrorist" operation in the village of Tarnac targeted a group of *anarcho-autonomes* who allegedly had taken part a few days earlier in a Black Bloc in Vichy, in addition to having attempted to stop trains from running by sabotaging the electric power supply.[46] The incident caused a sensation, and the accused were kept in jail for many months even though, in the end, the investigation was shown to be riddled with irregularities.[47] The misdeeds attributed to the *anarcho-autonomes* did not seem to warrant this level of attention; so noted a French jurist who observed that the most violent demonstrations in France today are held by "farmers."[48] Some wine growers have even engaged in clandestine actions involving the planting of bombs and the destruction of public buildings.[49] The goal of the police operation in Tarnac seemed to be above all political: to construct the image of an "ultra-leftist," an "interior enemy."[50] Hence, it is not the actions of Black Blocs so much as their radical ideas and rhetoric that give rise to massive repression.[51] This is by no means a new phenomenon.

In August 2001, Jürgen Storbeck, head of Interpol, declared that the so-called Black Bloc of anarchists can be regarded as "terrorists or pre-terrorists."[52] In the United States, the FBI has long viewed anarchist militants as potential "interior" terrorists, as indicated in reports submitted to Senate committees in 2001 and 2002.[53] In the aftermath of the attacks of September 11, 2001, at a meeting of the Working Party on Terrorism of the EU Council held on February 13, 2002, the noose began to tighten around anarchists and other radicals. According to a preparatory note, "the Working Party has noticed a gradual increase, at various European Union summits and other events, in violence and criminal damage orchestrated by radical extremist groups, clearly *terrorising* society."[54] More recently, during the anti-TAV demonstrations in Val di Susa, Italy, in the summer of 2011, the Minister of the Interior, Roberto Maroni, spoke of "violence with a terrorist signature."[55]

Radicalism has been equated with terrorism to discredit even certain actions less "violent" than those of some Black Blocs. Examples include French farmer and activist José Bové's "dismantling" of a McDonald's. Max Clos of the French daily *Le Figaro* mused on the similarity between Bové's direct action, carried out "on the pretext of fighting globalization," and the 9/11 attacks, before adding: "This is not, of course, on the same scale as the New York attacks, but it emanates from the same spirit." Bové as a clone of Osama bin Laden, no less![56] Journalists and commentators resort to the same sort of logic. In the United States, Michelle Malkin of *Capitalism Magazine* opines that "today's hollow-headed, rock-throwing, anti-capitalist puppeteers are tomorrow's John Walker Lindhs," in reference to the young American who joined the Taliban under the name Abdul Hamid and was captured by the US army when it invaded Afghanistan.[57] This equation is meant to point out to readers a supposedly logical connection between, say, a rock thrown at a bank window with no casualties and airliners sent crashing into New York skyscrapers with thousands of deaths as a result. The same theme is encountered in *Figaro Magazine,* where Alain Gérard Slama draws a link between the 9/11 attacks and the Black Blocs:

> It is difficult not to make the connection between the strike that has just shaken the Mecca of world capitalism and the hardening of the antiglobalization movements ... all of them adversaries of the liberal democratic state ... For the moment, the extreme-left vandals of the Black Blocs ... number only a few thousand. Only the blind can refuse to see how swiftly the malady is spreading.[58]

You would think Osama bin Laden and the Taliban's Mullah Omar had formed an affinity group and, wearing black hoodies, were circulating incognito among the Black Blocs.[59] In a similar vein, after four bombs exploded in London in July 2005—an attack carried out by Islamists to coincide with the G8 Summit in Scotland—Tim Dunn, the head of the political science department at the University of Exeter, published an article titled "Anarchists and Al-Qaeda." In it, he wondered "what distinguishes the violence used by Scottish anticapitalist anarchists from the tactics employed by Al-Qaeda in its attacks."[60] Yet the Black Blocs do *not* share the political and moral values of Islamist terrorists, nor (obviously) do they resort to the same means.

In Egypt, the BBC reported with regard to the Egyptian Black Bloc involved in mass protests against the Muslim Brotherhood government in January 2013 that

> the Muslim Brotherhood-affiliated TV channel, Misr 25, reported on 26 January that the Black Bloc was "part of the alleged revolution-ary movements, such as anarchism and the [Egyptian Trotskyist] Revolutionary Socialists. These movements reject the existence of a political, judicial or parliamentary system at all. They call for soci-eties without the state. In order to achieve this, they adopt all forms of violent and barbaric acts, such as killing and burning. These anarchic sabotage groups are not revolutionary groups. Rather, they use the revolution as a cover to cause chaos."[61]

Compared to an anarchist Black Bloc, a battalion of riot police in Cairo or elsewhere is far better equipped and far more violent. And consider here also the discipline and obedience the state imposes on its salaried defenders. Of the thousands of uniformed citizens deployed over the years to protect the major summits where leaders meet behind closed doors to discuss the modes of capitalist expansion, how many have shown the slightest hesitation, expressed the slightest democratic doubt? How many have refused to assault their fellow citizens? When they repeat the mantra that the "vandals" are just irrational "youths" who enter the fray solely out of a desire to "smash everything," spokes-people of the state, social democratic groups, and journalists are sim-ply fanning public hysteria and fuelling the demand for greater police violence against the "vandals." And in doing so, they are encouraging police obedience, fostering the police's contempt for the citizens in black, and promoting repressive violence.

In striving to dissociate themselves from the "rioters" at all costs and to deny them any political relevance, spokespersons for progres-sive organizations create a political vacuum around these "young vandals" and reinforce their social identification as deviant, mar-ginal elements. The police understand then that they are free to do as they wish, and all too often get carried away by their enthusiasm for repression, setting upon non-violent Black Blocs and brutalizing and arresting large numbers of peaceful protesters.

State Violence

The violence of the police response at the various summits and counter-summits has often been disproportionate to the Black Blocs' actions. The police are well aware that Black Blockers represent a marginal threat, that their political ideas are considered "deviant," and that they have no allies among the "respectable" political forces. Police deployments may be disproportionate, but they come with budgets and are profitable for police corps as well as for individual officers (in the form of overtime pay). There were 6,000 police officers in Quebec City for the 2001 Summit of the Americas (in addition to 500 soldiers kept in reserve); 16,000 police and soldiers at the EU Summit in Thessaloniki in 2003; 12,000 police at the 2005 G8 Summit in Scotland; 21,000 at the G8 Summit in Japan; 13,000 at the G8 Summit in Germany in 2007; 4,000 at the 2009 G20 Summit in Pittsburgh; respectively 10,000 and 14,000 French and German police at the 2009 NATO Summit in Strasbourg; 15,000 at the 2009 G8 Summit in Italy; 20,000 at the G8 and G20 Summits in Ontario in June 2010; and 10,000 at the G8 Summit in Deauville in May 2011.

The disproportionate police response is also apparent in the equipment used. The thousands of police mobilized for each major event are equipped with helmets, shields, padded fireproof uniforms, rubber bullet guns, smoke bombs, tear gas, and firearms, and supported by dogs, horses, armoured vehicles, sonic weapons, helicopters, prisons, and so forth. They can also count on the assistance of intelligence agencies and the military. In the repression that ensues, many protesters have sustained serious injuries, including broken skulls, arms, legs, and teeth. One night during the G8 Summit in Genoa, the Italian police stormed the Diaz school, where the Convergence Centre was located, and arrested all 91 individuals on the premises, about 60 of whom had to be removed in ambulances and taken directly to the hospital.[62] The number of arrests is also disproportionate: there were 601 in Seattle in 1999 (WTO meeting), and another 30 as a result of

Black Blockers face down a water cannon at the Quebec City protests against the Summit of the Americas, April 2001.

investigations after the events; 420 in Philadelphia in August 2000 (Republican National Convention); 859 in Prague in September 2000 (meeting of the IMF and World Bank); 463 in Quebec in April 2001 (Summit of the Americas); 539 in Göteborg in June 2001 (EU Summit); 329 arrested—and one killed—in Genoa in June 2001 (G8 Summit); 283 arrests in Miami in November 2003 (FTAA Summit); 1,821 in New York in Augusta and September 2004 (Republican Party Convention); 358 in Scotland in 2005 (G8 Summit); around 200 in Russia, ahead of the G8 Summit; 1,057 in Germany in 2007 (G8 Summit); 464 in Strasbourg in April 2009 (NATO Summit); 122 arrested—and one killed—in London in 2009 (G20 Summit); 190 in Pittsburgh in 2009 (G20 Summit); 1,200 in Copenhagen in November 2009 (Climate Change Summit); and 1,118 in Toronto in June 2010 (G20 Summit), with another 48 as a result of investigations after the events.[63]

What's more, the police do not hesitate to misinform the public by exaggerating the size of the "arsenals" found in the possession of Black

Blocs and their allies. This is very common when it comes to radical political groups. After demonstrations where arrests have been made, police forces stage an unveiling of the "spoils of war," and the media are invited to take pictures of a table where an impressive array of activist equipment is laid out. This was done in Italy in 2011 after demonstrations against the construction of a high-speed rail line in Val di Susa.[64] It is also a regular event in Montreal, and it occurred in Toronto after the 2010 G20 Summit. However, any attentive observer is likely to notice that the various objects on display tend to be inoffensive: staplers and scissors (for putting up posters), rattles, pans, cans, and drumsticks (to make music), sticks for holding up placards and banners, bullhorns, and even water bottles. The police endeavour to amplify the threat represented by protesters in general and Black Blocs in particular.[65] A rare occasion when journalists were not entirely taken in by the police was in Toronto after the G20 Summit; the police were forced to concede that a coat of mail and some arrows with padded heads had nothing to do with the demonstrations but belonged to an aficionado of medieval role playing who had been apprehended with his paraphernalia while on his way to meet fellow enthusiasts. The police had to make the same admission about a chainsaw and a crossbow that had also been seized. Several other "weapons" displayed turned out to be less than dangerous: "bandanas, skateboard and bicycle helmets, golf balls, tennis balls, goggles, rope and walkie-talkies."[66]

With the intention once again of manipulating public opinion, this time in the context of the protests against the IMF and World Bank in Washington, D.C., on April 16–17, 2000, the police declared that at the activists' Convergence Centre they had seized materials intended for fabricating pepper spray and Molotov cocktails. They later admitted that the pepper was actually meant as an ingredient for gazpacho and that the bottles were plastic. In Montreal on April 26, 2002, in the wake of mass arrests made before a march protesting a preparatory meeting of the G8 labour ministers could get under way, police spokesman André Durocher resorted to the same ruse, holding up plastic bottles for the cameras and claiming they were Molotov cocktails. Now, a Molotov cocktail is a gasoline-filled bottle with a burning wick; for it to work, it must shatter upon landing, so it must be made of glass. This police fabrication should perhaps be dubbed a "Durocher cocktail," since its sole purpose was to inflame public opinion and reduce to ashes the credibility of social movements. The same Durocher also stated that one of the people arrested had been in possession of a pistol. This happened to be true, but only days later did the police reveal that the individual in question had no connection with the protesters. In 2002, during demonstrations in Washington again targeting the IMF and World Bank, the police declared that they had seized some bombs that demonstrators had been carrying. The next day the police admitted there had been no bombs. At the G8 Summit in Genoa in July 2001, the Italian police, who in the middle of the night had brutally cleared the Convergence Centre, declared that they had found Molotov cocktails there. Many months later, testifying before a public inquiry, they admitted to having placed the Molotov cocktails in the building themselves. In Philadelphia, during mobilizations against the Republican Party Convention, a police commander claimed to have seized explosives and acid-filled balloons in a warehouse where activists were in fact building giant puppets. During the same event, the police also announced that they had intercepted a van transporting poisonous snakes and reptiles, which were to be let loose in the streets. The van actually belonged to a pet shop owner. The police also asserted that officers had been splashed with acid and that "dry ice bombs" had been found in the city. None of these stories were true.[67] In sum, the police magnify the threat represented by protesters to justify repression and, in some cases, mass arrests. By the time the false statements are corrected, public interest in the events has waned and journalists show little interest in the new information.

Repression can be lethal. In Göteborg, the police fired real bullets and seriously injured a number of demonstrators. In Genoa, Carlo Giuliani—who was not wearing black—waved a fire extinguisher in the direction of a police vehicle; in response, an officer killed him with two bullets to the head at point-blank range. The police jeep then drove twice over his motionless body. Yet the next day, the G8 heads of state spoke out against the "blind violence" of the *demonstrators;*

and meanwhile, non-violent progressives, generally so quick to distance themselves from the "vandals," apparently had no qualms about appropriating the memory of Carlo Giuliani, hailing him as a martyr to the common cause. In London in 2009, during the G20 Summit, a bystander died of cardiac arrest after being clubbed by a police officer.

In the early 2000s, the World Development Movement, in its study of demonstrations held in developing countries specifically to denounce decisions made by the IMF and World Bank, concluded that dozens of people had been killed by the police or armed forces and that those injured or arrested numbered in the thousands.[68] Here are two specific cases. In February 2001, four people, including a 14-year-old, were killed in the Ecuadorian Amazon when the army dispersed a demonstration of indigenous people involved in a campaign against a restructuring plan drawn up by the IMF (whereby 50 percent of the national budget would be earmarked to pay down the country's debt). And in Argentina in 2001, some 30 demonstrators were killed during a wave of protests against that country's economic and financial crisis. Because journalists in the West were completely ignorant of these massacres, they felt free to unanimously describe the killing of Carlo Giuliani as, to quote France 2 (July 21, 2001), "the first death in history of an anti-globalization protester."

The companies that manufacture and sell anti-protester weapons refer to repressive efficiency when vaunting the quality of their wares. For instance, pictures taken at the 2010 G20 Summit in Toronto were used for promotional purposes by Mawashi, a manufacturer of police protective gear.[69] That company also uses the pictures on its website, where there are references to alter-globalization demonstrators: "13,000 officers deployed at the 2007 G8 Summit in Germany; 433 injured. How do you know if your Riot Gear is up to the task? If it has CSA Z617 Impact Protection then be confident it is."[70] The website of Police Ordnance, an Ontario-based maker and distributor of weapons that were employed in Quebec City in April 2001, offered what amounted to an ode to repression. The text commended the RCMP and the SQ for their excellent work in containing several hundred violent demonstrators, boasting that tear gas had dissuaded most of the would-be troublemakers, while the others were easy targets for rubber bullets fired with the company's ARWEN37 and ARWENACE guns. Besides extolling the company's products, the website quoted its on-site observers, who congratulated the police in Quebec City for their high level of professionalism.[71] Thus, in the absurd world denounced by anti-capitalist demonstrators, their own repression serves as a sales pitch for the very weapons used to repress them.

On the ground, the Black Bloc battalions and those of the uniformed citizens paid by the state embody two visions of the world, two diametrically opposed conceptions of human beings: on the far left, free and equal individuals; on the far right, obedient and unequal individuals. Meanwhile, today's public discourse muddles the mind and distorts reality, to the point that many people associate protesters with madness and chaos, and the police with freedom and equality. The onlookers, effectively deceived and frightened by this discourse,

Black Blockers and other protesters return the police volley of tear gas canisters during the Summit of the Americas in Quebec City, April 2001.

applaud when they hear that, having violently dispersed the protesters, the supporters of authority and hierarchy, of law and order, continue to hold sway now and always.

At the end of the previous edition of this book, published in French in 2007, I wrote: "It is true that the media are paying less attention to this tactic [the Black Bloc], that mass demonstrations—which actually are often less massive than before—take place in a somewhat different environment, one that blurs the significance of tactics of direct confrontation and tends to restrict the latitude available to activists." In other words, I felt this tactic was not as relevant, in terms of politics and activism, as it had been a few years earlier. I nevertheless concluded with this quotation from Daniel Dylan Young:

> Whether the Black Bloc continues as a tactic or is abandoned, it certainly has served its purpose. In certain places and times the Black Bloc effectively empowered people to take action in collective solidarity against the violence of state and capitalism. It is important that we neither cling to it nostalgically as an outdated ritual or tradition, nor reject it wholesale because it sometimes seems inappropriate. Rather we should continue working pragmatically to fulfill our individual needs and desires through various tactics and objectives, as they are appropriate at the specific moment. Masking up in Black Bloc has its time and place, as do other tactics which conflict with it.[72]

Since then, the economic crisis has worsened and the political crisis along with it. I took part in the demonstrations against the G20 Summit in Toronto in 2010 and those organized during the student strike in Quebec in 2012. I engaged with other anarchists in discussions about their recent experiences, in Canada and elsewhere, and, in preparing this new edition, I immersed myself once again in Black Bloc statements and communiqués, pictures and videos, debates and newspaper articles. And I have arrived at the conclusion that, to borrow a slogan

"We Are All Black Bloc!" G20 solidarity protest, Clark Drive, Vancouver, Canada, July 4, 2010.

from the rebellions in Greece, the Black Bloc is perhaps "an image of the future." And by way of an echo, Italian anarchists have said of the Black Blocs, "We are the future you should listen to, the only healthy part of a country plagued with metastases."[73]

APPENDIX

Some Black Blocs of the Alter-Globalization Movement (1999–2010)

- Seattle, November 30, 1999. WTO Summit. Far from the demonstrations, a Black Bloc about 250 strong targets capitalist symbols in the city's shopping district.
- Washington, D.C., April 16, 2000. Meeting of the IMF and the World Bank. The Black Bloc directs its efforts toward protecting non-violent demonstrations against police assaults.
- Prague, September 2000. Meeting of the IMF and the World Bank. A Black Bloc armed with clubs, rocks, and Molotov cocktails confronts a police barrage in a failed attempt to force its way through to the convention centre.
- Quebec City, April 2001. Summit of the Americas. Several small Black Blocs harass the security perimeter and the police officers assigned to it, at the same time protecting other demonstrators against police attacks.
- Göteborg, May 2001. EU Summit. A Black Bloc confronts the police, who fire real bullets at the crowd.
- Genoa, June 2001. G8 Summit. The Black Blocs and their allies strike symbols of capitalism, attack a prison, and retaliate when assaulted by the police. A police officer kills a demonstrator with two gunshots to the head.
- Calgary, June 2002. G8 Summit (at Kananaskis). A Black Bloc of several dozen people engages in a peaceful march.
- Prague, November 21, 2002. NATO Summit. Recognizing a provocation, a Black Bloc manoeuvres to protect a police vehicle slowly making its way through a rally of some 3,000 anarcho-communists.
- Geneva/Annemasse, May 2003. G8 Summit (in Évian). A Black Bloc about 100 strong takes independent action in Geneva, suddenly appearing late in the evening in the downtown shopping area when everything is quiet, hurling stones and Molotov cocktails at the shop windows, then vanishing a few minutes later. Over the following days, Black Blocs together with other groups of demonstrators engage in street-blocking actions (preventing access to Summit meeting places).
- Thessaloniki, June 2003. EU Summit. Black Blocs participate in street-blocking actions and battle police officers protecting the Summit. The next day they demonstrate in the city alongside tens of thousands of other protesters

and attack capitalist symbols. They set fire to a McDonald's and a Vodafone store and wreck some 30 other establishments, including three banks.

- Cancun, September 2003. WTO Summit. A Black Bloc takes part in a skirmish around the security fence, alongside activists of the women's and peasants' movements. (A South Korean peasant commits suicide to protest against indebtedness.)
- Miami, November 2003. Summit of the Americas. A Black Bloc takes part in the rally, trying in vain to protect some giant puppets from the police.
- Auchterarder, Scotland, June 2005. G8 Summit. A Black Bloc undertakes a "Suicide March" to draw the police away from the many affinity groups.
- Heiligendamm–Rostock, June 2007. G8 Summit. A huge Black Bloc participates in the rallies against the Summit. The following day, it attempts without success to spark a riot in a gentrified neighbourhood of East Berlin (an action called Plan B).
- London, April 2009. G20 Summit. A Black Bloc joins demonstrations against the Summit, smashing bank windows. (A passerby is clubbed by a police officer and subsequently dies of a heart attack.)
- Pittsburgh, September 2009. G20 Summit. A small Black Bloc participating in rallies against the Summit engages in minor confrontations with the police.
- Toronto, June 2010. G20 Summit. A Black Bloc joins the large unitary march. After several attempts to breach police lines and approach the security fence, it breaks away from the demonstration and dashes along some commercial streets, breaking dozens of windows before dispersing.
- Chicago, June 2012. NATO Summit. A Black Bloc of about 100 attempts to break through police lines. The police resort to force to stop them.

NOTES

Notes to Introduction

Epigraphs: Nicolas Tavaglione, "Qui a peur de l'homme noir?", *Le Courrier* (Geneva), June 11, 2003, 4; Interview in "Toronto: Le Black Bloc passe à l'action," *Casse sociale* 5 (2010):16.

1   Jeff Shantz, *Active Anarchy: Political Practice in Contemporary Movements* (Lanham: Lexington Books, 2011), 52.

2   See, for example, Patrick Tillard, "Une affection bâclée," *Divergences* (August 2006): 6. Web. Tillard also criticizes what he considers the theoretical weakness of the analysis of the Black Bloc phenomenon put forward in the first edition of this book; he takes the opportunity (in the far left's justifiable tradition of mistrusting academics) to insult me and accuse me of offering a "parasitic reading" of the Black Blocs, whose struggle, he suggests, I wish to co-opt for my own benefit and for the benefit of reformist forces.

3   Author's interview with BB3, in 2002. To protect the anonymity of my interviewees, I have not identified them by name. At the time of the interview, BB3 was 23 years old, and she had participated in Black Blocs at rallies against a G20 meeting in Montreal in November 2000, against police brutality in Montreal on March 15, 2001, and against the Summit of the Americas in Quebec City in April 2001.

4   Mike Mowbray, "Blogging the Greek Riots: Between Aftermath and Ongoing Engagement," *Resistance Studies* 1 (2012).

5   Interview in "Toronto: Le Black Bloc passe à l'action," 14. Our translation.

6   Stephen Moss, "Black Bloc: 'Only Actions Count Now,'" *The Guardian*, March 31, 2011. Web.

7   BB2, interviewed by the author in September 2002. BB2 was twenty-two years old at the time of the interview. He had taken part in Black Blocs during a march in Westmount (a posh Montreal neighbourhood) on May 1, 2000; at a protest rally against a G20 meeting in Montreal in November 2000; and at a demonstration opposing the Summit of the Americas in Quebec City in April 2001.

8   Amory Starr, "'(Excepting barricades erected to prevent us from peacefully assembling)': So-called 'violence' in the global North alterglobalization movement," *Social Movement Studies* 5, no. 1 (May 2006): 70–71.

9   Severino, "Has the Black Bloc tactic reached the end of its usefulness?", *Common Struggle / Lucha Común*, November 18, 2002. Web.

10 CrimethInc., "Black Bloc: A primer," *Profane Existence* 43 (Summer–Fall 2003): 10.

11 See *A-Infos,* September 28, 2003. Web.

12 Robert Booth and Marc Vallé, "'Black Bloc' anarchists behind anti-cuts rampage reject thuggery claims," *The Guardian* (London), April 1, 2001. Web.

13 *Schwabe and M.G. v. Germany,* European Court of Human Rights, 5th Section (November 8, 2011), 2 (§9).

14 Florian Gathmann, Jan Grundmann, and Philipp Wittrock, "Anarchists in Europe: What unites the stone-throwing Black Bloc?", *Spiegel International,* November 12, 2008. Web.

15 See "Behind the mask: Violence and representational politics," *Upping the Anti* 11 (n.d.). Web.

16 Don Peat and Jonathan Jenkins, "And now the cleanup," *Toronto Sun,* June 28, 2010, 12; Joe Fiorito, "Wisdom from the Sunday pulpit," *Toronto Star,* June 28, 2010, GT2.

17 Kenneth Kidd, "Tear gas fired in rampage," *Toronto Star,* June 27, 2010, A6; Curtis Rush, "Retiring deputy chief calls G20 reaction overblown," *Toronto Star,* August 12, 2011. Some believe the police voluntarily abandoned some of their vehicles to the angry crowd in order to later justify the repression. See, for instance, Arnaud Montreuil, "L'acceptation silencieuse des Québécois: Arrestations du G20," *Le Devoir* (Montreal), July 7, 2010, A7.

18 "Riot recap: Our bloggers chronicle," *Toronto Star,* June 28, 2010, GT1.

19 Canadian Press, "Toronto strip club among businesses reimbursed after G20," CBC, October 30, 2012. Web.

20 Kidd, "Tear gas."

21 Kidd, "Tear gas."

22 "Black Bloc anarchists emerge," BBC, February 1, 2013. Web.

23 Kayla Young, "Words behind the mask: The 'encapuchados' of Chile's education movement," *I Love Chile,* October 25, 2011. Web.

24 Dave Abel et al., "Organized anarchy," *Toronto Sun,* June 27, 2010, 4.

25 Visit http://www.cartacapital.com.br. ("O Black Bloc, forma de protesto antissistema, usa a depredação de bancos e fachadas de grandes empresas como meio de atuação. O que você acha? (1) Sou contra qualquer tipo de vandalismo, em qualquer hipótese. (2) No caso de determinadas empresas, desde que ninguém seja ferido, sou a favor.") Thanks to Geneviève Pagé for help with the translation.

26 Thanks to Geneviève Pagé for help with the translation.

27 Thanks to Eve-Marie Lampron for help with the translation.

28 Inés Santaeulalia, "Grupos anarquistas, la mano que creo el caos en la Ciudad de México," *El Pais,* December 2, 2012, M2. Web.

29 Kathryn Blaze Carlson, "The Black Bloc: A look at the anarchists who could be the biggest G20 security threat," *National Post,* June 14, 2010. Web.

30 Louis-Gilles Francœur, "Les gyrophares dans la forêt," *Le Devoir* (Montreal), June 22, 2012. Web. Our translation.

31 Daryl Lindsey, "The world from Berlin: Putin, Leader of the G-8's Black Bloc," *Spiegel International,* June 6, 2007. Web.

32 Gord Hill, *The Anti-Capitalist Resistance Comic Book* (Vancouver: Arsenal Pulp, 2012).

33 Here is an excerpt appearing on the back cover of the novel *Une fièvre impossible à négocier* by Lola Lafon (Paris: Flammarion, 2003): "Then, just as I was about to fall forever, a few Black Stars take hold of me on either side, gripping my arms. We are a chain. Solidary, a block, a Black Bloc." Our translation.

34 *Black Block,* visit http://www.blackblock.org.

35 "Black Bloc Portraits series," *Indymedia* (Washington), January 24, 2005. Web.

36 Robert Klaten et al., eds., *Art and Agenda: Political Art and Activism* (Berlin: Gestalten, 2011), 33. Also, visit http://www.youtube.com/watch?v=p3EDmVbnvzI.

37 Jérôme Montes, "Mouvements anti-mondialisation: la crise de la démocratie representative," *Études internationales* 33, no. 4 (December 2001).

38 Francesco Alberti, "Maalox e ammoniaca: La guerriglia dei black bloc," *Corriere Della Sera* (Milan), July 4, 2011, p. 3. Thanks to E.-M. Lampron for the translation.

39 Jonathan Brown, "Recriminations fly after anti-cuts protests descend into violence," *The Independent* (London), March 28, 2011.

40 Laurent Mossu, "Des casseurs sèment la terreur à Genève et Lausanne," *Le Figaro* (Paris), June 2, 2003. Our translation.

41 "'José Bové viendra!' La police aussi," *Courrier international,* April 11, 2001. Our translation.

42 Federal Office of the Police, Federal Department of Justice and the Police, Analysis and Prevention Service, "Le potentiel de violence résidant dans le mouvement antimondialisation," Berne, July 2001. My thanks to Olivier Fillieule for pointing out this source. Our translation.

43 Rob Granatstein, "Mistreated by cops in riot? Tough luck," *Toronto Sun,* June 28, 2010, 19.

44 Alan Travis, "Cuts protest: Theresa May to review police powers in aftermath of clashes," *The Guardian* (London), March 28, 2011. Web.

45 Brown, "Recriminations fly."

46   Ashley Terry et al., "More than 300 protesters charged amidst violent G20 protests," *Vancouver Sun*, June 27, 2010. Web.

47   Quoted in "Verhofstadt et Prodi déplorent la mort d'un manifestant à Gênes," AFP, July 20, 2001. Our translation.

48   Frédéric Garlan, "Les Huit ne se laisseront pas intimider par les casseurs," AFP, July 23, 2001. Our translation.

49   Garlan, "Les Huit."

50   Donatella della Porta and Lorenzo Zamponi, "Protest and policing on October 15th, global day of action: the Italian case," *Policing and Society* 23, no. 1 (2013): 65–68.

51   Mark Hume, "Riot investigators overwhelmed by Internet leads," *Globe and Mail,* August 24, 2012. Web.

52   "Vancouver police shift blame for riot," CBC, June 20, 2011. Web.

53   "1. Mai in Berlin: Die Stunde der Krawall-Idioten," *Berlin Kurier*, May 1, 2012. Web. Thanks to BB6 for the translation.

54   A right-wing think tank concerned with "terrorism, political extremism, warfare and organized crime."

55   Granatstein, "Mistreated by cops."

56   Blaze, "The Black Bloc."

57   *The World in Your Hands.* Visit http://www.aljazeera.net/news/pages/43c2d261-a6a1-4dd0-90b7-b3ad0afaf88b. Thanks to Vincent Romani for help with the translation.

58   Pierre Celerier, "Les manifestants contre le FMI jouent au chat et à la souris avec la police," AFP, April 16, 2000. Our translation.

59   "Manifestation pacifique de plus de 30000 personnes dans les rues de Québec," AFP, April 21, 2001. Our translation.

60   Celerier, "Les manifestants."

61   "Affrontements entre policiers et manifestants en marge du sommet de Göteborg," *Le Monde,* AFP, June 15, 2001. Our translation.

62   Christian Spillmann, "Gênes: violences, discorde, les dirigeants du G8 n'ont pas de quoi pavoiser," AFP, July 22, 2001. Our translation.

63   Televised news reports, TF1, July 20–21, 2001. Our translation.

64   Dominique Lagarde et al., "Black Blocs: les casseurs de l'antimondialisa-tion," *L'Express*, September 6, 2001. Our translation.

65   Sébastien Blanc, "Gênes achève le G8 complètement groggy," AFP, July 22, 2001. Our translation.

66   Sébastien Blanc, "La violence des anti-G8 radicaux déferle sur Gênes," AFP, July 20, 2001. Our translation.

67   José Carron, "Insaisissables, les Black Blocs effraient et fascinent," *La Tribune de Genève*, June 2, 2003, 5. Our translation.

68 Mark Townsend et al., "Anti-cuts march draws hundreds of thousands as police battle rioters," *The Guardian*, March 27, 2011. Web.

69 "Home secretary Theresa May condemns protest 'thugs,'" BBC, March 28, 2011. Web.

70 Chris Hedges, "The cancer in Occupy," *Truthdig*, February 6, 2012. Web. For a defence of the Oakland Black Bloc, see Aragorn!, ed., "The Anti-Capitalist March and the Black Bloc," *Occupy Everything! Anarchists in the Occupy Movement 2009–2011* (LBC, 2012), 161–69.

71 For a presentation of responses on the left and far left following Black Bloc actions in Toronto in 2010, see the excellent dossier Xrednick, "La gauche, la casse et le Black Bloc," *Casse Sociale* 5 (2010): 17–43. On the subject of Jack Layton, see Ashley Terry, Linda Nguyen, Mark Kennedy, and Carmen Chai, "More than 300 protesters charged amidst violent G20 protests." Web.

72 Christian Losson, "Des antimondialistes dans la tactique de l'affrontement: des mouvements anars radicalisent la contestation," *Libération*, June 18, 2001. Our translation. See also Susan George and Martin Wolf, *La Mondialisation libérale* (Paris: Bernard Grasset-Les Échos, 2002), 167.

73 "Prospects for revolution: Canadian perspectives 2011," *Fightback: The Marxist Voice of Labour and Youth*, April 11, 2011. Web.

74 Léonce Aguirre, "'Black Bloc,' violences et intoxication," *Rouge*, June 5, 2003.

75 Joe Fiorito, "Wisdom from the Sunday pulpit," *Toronto Star*, June 28, 2010, GT2.

76 There are a few exceptional cases of journalists discussing the political motivations of the Black Blocs, even to the point of referring to communiqués put out on the Internet. One example is an article signed Ad. G., "Qui sont les hommes masqués et pourquoi leur révolte?" *La Tribune de Genève*, June 2, 2003, 5. See also Moss, "Black Bloc."

77 I was able to observe the Black Blocs directly on various occasions, including the following demonstrations: against the official visit of Front national representatives in Montreal on September 22, 1993; against the American Free Trade Zone project discussed at the Summit of the Americas in Quebec City in April 2001; against the World Economic Forum in New York in January and February of 2002; against the G8 Summit in Calgary in July 2002; against the G20 Summit in Toronto in 2010; and during the Quebec Student Strike in 2012 (specifically, the Victoriaville riot, among other events).

78 A number of these were reproduced in the first French edition of this book, *Les Black Blocs: La Liberté et l'égalité se manifestent* (Montreal: Lux, 2003).

Notes to Chapter 1

1   "Suffragettes riot, 112 arrested," *New York Times*, June 30, 1909.
2   Emmeline Pankhurst, *My Own Story* (London: Eveleigh Nash, 1912), 12.
3   Andrew Rosen, *Rise Up, Women!* (London: Routledge and Kegan Paul, 1974), 189.
4   C.J. Bearman, "An examination of suffragette violence," *English Historical Review* 120, no. 486 (2005): 365–97; June Purvis, "'Deeds, not words': The daily lives of militant suffragettes in Edwardian Britain," *Women's Studies International Forum* 18, no. 2 (1995): 91–101; Martha Vicinus, "Male Space and Women's Bodies: The English Suffragette Movement," in *Women in Culture and Politics: A Century of Change*, ed. Judith Friedlander et al. (Bloomington: Indiana University Press, 1986), 209–22.
5   Virginia Woolf, *Three Guineas (Annotated)*, ed. Mark Hussey, introduced and annotated by Jane Marcus (Boston: Harcourt, 2006), 175.
6   Richard A. Rempel, Andrew Brink, and Margaret Moran, eds., *The Collected Papers of Bertrand Russell*, vol. 12 (London: Allen and Unwin, 1985), 244; Brian Harrison, "Bertrand Russell: The False Consciousness of a Feminist," *Russell: The Journal of Bertrand Russell Studies* 4, no. 1 (1984): 177.
7   David Van Deusen, "The Emergence of the Black Bloc and the Movement Towards Anarchism," in *The Black Blocs Papers: An Anthology of Primary Texts from the North American Black Bloc 1999–2001*, ed. David Van Deusen and Xavier Massot (Green Mountain Anarchist Collective) (Baltimore: Black Clover, 2002), 14.
8   See Dan Berger, *Outlaws of America: The Weather Underground and the Politics of Solidarity* (Oakland: AK, 2006).
9   *Comme un indien métropolitain : SCALP 1984–1992* (Paris: Réseau No Pasaran, 2005), esp. 45.
10 Not to be confused with "autonomist" movements, which strive for the recognition of a distinct national or regional culture.
11 Mention should be made of Italy's Autonomia movement of the 1960s and 1970s, whose members were far-left working-class and youth activists critical of the official Communist Party. For an intellectual history of the Italian Autonomia movement, see Steve Wright, *Storming Heaven: Class Composition and Struggle in Italian Autonomist Marxism* (London: Pluto, 2002).
12 George Katsiaficas, "The necessity of autonomy," *New Political Science* 23, no. 4 (2001): 547–53.
13 Barbara Michaud, "L'anarchisme n'est pas un individualisme: l'exemple des squats," *Argument* 3, no. 1 (2000): 110–15.

14   A.G. Grauwacke, *Autonome in Bewegung: Aus den Ersten 23 Jahren* (Berlin: Assoziation A, 2003).

15   Sina Rahmani, "Macht kaputt was euch kaputt macht: On the history and the meaning of the Black Block," *Politics and Culture* 4 (November 9, 2009). Web.

16   Franco Fracassi, *Black Bloc: Viaggio nel pianeta nero* (Lecco: Studio, 2011), 25–26.

17   Rahmani, "Macht kaputt."

18   Rahmani, "Macht kaputt."

19   BB4, interviewed by the author in Montreal on November 26, 2003. A resident of Amsterdam, he was 42 years old at the time and had participated in Black Blocs during the 1980s and in the squat movement in Germany and the Netherlands. See also "Solidarity with Hafenstrasse," *Open Road* 19 (Summer 1986): 3.

20   This account of the origins of the Black Blocs is indebted to George Katsiaficas, *The Subversion of Politics: European Autonomous Social Movements and the Decolonization of Everyday Life* (New Jersey: Humanities Press International, 1997), which has been summarized and presented in an international perspective in Daniel Dylan Young, "Autonomia and the Origin of the Black Bloc," visit *A-Infos*. See also the section "Movement Use of Violence" in Chapter 5 of Anders Corr, *No Trespassing: Squatting, Rent Strikes, and Land Struggles Worldwide* (Boston: South End, 1999); and Donatella della Porta, "Protest, Protesters, and Protest Policing: Public Discourses in Italy and Germany from the 1960s to the 1980s," in *How Social Movements Matter*, ed. Marco Giugni, Doug McAdam, and Charles Tilly (Minneapolis. University of Minnesota Press, 1999): 66–96.

21   Florian Gathmann, Jan Grundmann, and Philipp Wittrock, "Anarchists in Europe—What unites the stone-throwing Black Bloc?", *Spiegel International*, November 12, 2008. Web.

22   BB6, interview with the author. BB6 is a pro-feminist man who took part in the Quebec student movement and the anti-capitalist, anti-fascist, anti-racist movement in Germany from 2009 to 2012.

23   Charles Tilly, "Les origines du répertoire d'action collective contemporaine en France et en Grande-Bretagne," *Vingtième siècle* 4 (October 1984): 89–108; Doug McAdam and Dieter Rucht, "The cross-national diffusion of Movement ideas," *Annals of the American Academy of Political and Social Sciences* 528 (July 1993): 56–74.

24   See, for example, Jeremy, "Letter from the Berlin squats," *Love and Rage* 2, no. 4 (April 1991): 12; Anarchist Youth Federation, "We're pro-choice and we're riot," *Love and Rage* 3, no. 4 (April–May 1992): 12; Ickibob, "On the Black Bloc," *Love and Rage* (July–August 1992), reprinted in Roy San

Filippo, *A New World in Our Hearts: Eight Years of Writings from the Love and Rage Revolutionary Anarchist Federation* (Oakland: AK, 2003), 39–40.

25 David Graeber, "Concerning the violent peace-police: An open letter to Chris Hedges," *N+1*, February 9, 2012. Web.

26 The first Indymedia centre was established on the occasion of the Battle of Seattle. It brought together students, community workers, and activists. Since then a host of cities have acquired Indymedia websites. These operate on an open publishing basis—that is, anyone can publish texts and images on them directly. Although not entirely devoted to alter-globalization, the Indymedia network remains one of the most useful resources for obtaining details on alter-globalization rallies.

27 Alan O'Connor, "Punk subculture in Mexico and the anti-globalization movement: A report from the front," *New Political Science* 25, no. 1 (2003): 43–53.

28 According to BB3.

29 A.K. Thompson, *Black Bloc White Riot: Anti-Globalization and the Genealogy of Dissent* (Oakland: AK, 2010).

30 Elizabeth "Betita" Martinez, "Where was the colour in Seattle? Looking for reasons why the Great Battle was so white," *Colorlines* 3, no. 1 (Spring 2000). Web.

31 Geoffrey Pleyers, "Des Black Blocs aux alter-activistes: pôles et formes d'engagement des jeunes altermondialistes," *Lien social et politiques* 51 (Spring 2004): 125–26.

32 Mark LeVine, "The revolution, back in black," *Aljazeera*, February 2, 2013. Web.

33 Mary Black, "Letter from inside the Black Bloc," June 24, 2001. Web.

34 See David Tough's critique, "The civil rights movement and the Black Bloc," *Upping the Anti* 12 (2011): 12.

35 Stephen Moss, "Black Bloc: 'Only Actions Count Now,'" *The Guardian*, March 31, 2011. Web.

36 Robert Booth and Marc Vallé, "'Black Bloc' anarchists behind anti-cuts rampage reject thuggery claims," *The Guardian* (London), April 1, 2001. Web.

37 Centre des médias alternatifs du Québec (CMAQ), "Manifeste du Carré Noir." Web. Our translation.

38 ACME Collective, "N30 Black Bloc communiqué," December 4, 1999. Web.

39 This is confirmed in Van Deusen, "The Emergence of the Black Bloc," 15.

40 The same deliberation process can be seen at work in the decision of European squatters to adopt more aggressive methods of struggle. See Corr, "Movement use of violence?", in Corr, *No Trespassing*.

41 BB2, interview with the author. Our translation. The same observation was made by French militants in Clément Barette, *La pratique de la violence*

politique par l'émeute: le cas de la violence exercée lors des contre-sommets (M.A. thesis, Université de Paris I—Panthéon-Sorbonne, 2002), 93.

42 For an in-depth discussion of affinity groups, see Francis Dupuis-Déri, "Anarchism and the politics of affinity groups," *Anarchist Studies* 18, no. 1 (2010).

43 Interview published as "Toronto: Le Black Bloc passe à l'action," *Casse sociale* 5 (2010): 15.

44 BB7, a 26-year-old woman interviewed in Montreal in 2013. As a resident of a small town in Quebec, she discovered the Black Blocs while watching TV reports on the student strike of 2005, at which point she began to take part in demonstrations, eventually joining various Black Blocs during the 2012 student strike.

45 Interview with GA7, conducted in Paris in June 2003. Female, age 24. Boston resident. Took part in her first affinity group in 2001 during the occupation of Harvard administration offices to demand better working conditions for the superintendents. Participated in other groups during rallies against the World Economic Forum in New York (winter of 2002), against the war in Iraq (in Boston in 2003), and against the G8 in France (June 2003).

46 The impossibility of preventing informal power from being exercised is no doubt the most commonly heard criticism of anarchism. Anarchists and other anti-authoritarians, such as the radical feminists of the 1970s, have examined this issue and proposed various solutions. On the problem of informal power, see, for example, Jo Freeman, "The Tyranny of Structurelessness," in *Quiet Rumours: An Anarcha-Feminist Reader*, ed. Dark Star (Oakland: AK, 2012), 68–75. For a recent examination of authority in anarchist groups, see Philippe Coutant, "L'autorité dans les groupes militants, les groupes libertaires?", *Les Temps maudits* 12 (2001). Web. This text proposes solutions and procedures to reduce the inequality of informal powers. Another that does so is Morjane Baba, *Guérilla Kit: ruses et techniques des nouvelles luttes anticapitalistes* (Paris: La Découverte, 2003), 151–61. Still another is Per Herngren, *Path of Resistance: The Practice of Civil Disobedience* (Philadelphia: New Society, 1993), 149–92.

47 ACME Collective, "N30 Black Bloc communiqué."

48 Lesley J. Wood, "Breaking the bank and taking to the streets," *Journal of World-Systems Research* 10, no. 1 (2004): 3–23.

49 In *Après avoir tout brûlé … Suite au Sommet de l'OTAN à Strasbourg en avril 2009—correspondance à propos de stratégies et émotions révolutionnaires*, 5. Web.

50 Quoted by the Wu Ming collective in "Stop The Encirclement of the Black Bloc." Web.

51   In Barette, *La pratique de la violence politique*, 103, 105. Our translation. On the subject of activists' concern with not endangering other demonstrators, see also Amory Starr, "'(Excepting barricades erected to prevent us from peacefully assembling)': So-called 'violence' in the global North alterglobalization movement," *Social Movement Studies* 5, no. 1 (May 2006): 70–71. See also Van Deusen, "The Emergence of the Black Bloc," 18.

52   David Graeber, *Possibilities: Essays on Hierarchy, Rebellion, and Desire* (Oakland: AK, 2007), 390.

53   "Les poings rouges: l'organisation des communistes dans les manifestations de rue," *Socialisme maintenant!*, été 2001, 15. Our translation.

54   Excerpts from an interview with a member of the Tute Bianche who took part in the demonstrations in Prague in September 2000, quoted in Starr, "'(Excepting barricades ...),'" 68.

55   Antonio Negri and Michael Hardt, *Multitude: War and Democracy in the Age of Empire* (New York: Penguin, 2004), 264–67; Samizdat.net, ed., *Gênes, 19–20–21 juillet 2001, multitudes en marche contre l'Empire* (Paris: Éditions REFLEX, 2002).

56   For more information on this form of collective action, visit "ROR London," *Rhythms of Resistance*. Web.

57   See George McKay, ed., *DIY Culture: Party and Protest in Nineties Britain* (London: Verso, 1998), 15. In the same volume, see also John Jordan, "The Art of Necessity: The Subversive Imagination of Anti-Road Protest and Reclaim the Streets," 129–51.

58   See David Graeber, "The new anarchists," *New Left Review* 2, no. 13 (January–February 2002): 66–68.

59   Karen Goaman, "The Anarchist Travelling Circus: Reflections on Contemporary Anarchism, Anti-Capitalism, and the International Scene," in *Changing Anarchism: Anarchist Theory and Practice in a Global Age*, ed. Jonathan Purkis and James Bowen (Manchester: Manchester University Press, 2004), 164.

60   Kolonel Klepto and Major Up Evil, "The Clandestine Insurgent Rebel Clown Army Goes to Scotland via a Few Other Places," in *Shut Them Down! The G8, Gleneagles 2005 and the Movement of Movements*, ed. David Harvie et al. (West Yorkshire and New York: Dissent! G8/Autonomedia, 2005), 243–54.

61   Visit http://www.clownarmy.org/index.html.

62   Written information, photos, and videos accessed at "Strasbourg: témoignage de la clown army," Web; "Solidaires contre le cirque sécuritaire," Web; and "OTAN: Défilé de clowns et escarmouches à Strasbourg," Web.

63   Clare Solomon and Tania Palmieri, eds., *Springtime: The New Student Rebellions* (London: Verso, 2011), 110–21.

64 Harvie et al., *Shut Them Down!*, 243–54.
65 See "Lausanne: des blacks & pinks témoignent et revendiquent." Web.
66 Krystalline Kraus, "Sisters in struggle," *rabble.ca*, June 21, 2002. Web. Another source was the account heard by the author from a feminist friend who witnessed the event first-hand.
67 This Pink Bloc, with scarcely a handful of members, stole the show and made the front page of *La Presse* (Montreal), March 8, 2004.
68 Regarding a demonstration in London where the police brutally set upon protesters, see Steve Reicher, "The Battle of Westminster: Developing the social identity model of crowd behaviour in order to deal with the initiation and development of collective conflict," *European Journal of Social Psychology* 26 (1996): 115–34; and Steve Reicher et al., "A Model of Crowd Prototypes and Crowd Leadership," in *Leadership and Social Movements*, ed. Colin Barker, Alan Johnson, and Michael Lavalette (Manchester: Manchester University Press, 2001).
69 Though not an anarchist, the political philosopher Hannah Arendt articulates the same position in *Crises of the Republic: Lying in Politics, Civil Disobedience, On Violence, Thoughts on Politics and Revolution* (New York: Houghton Mifflin Harcourt, 1972), 49–102.

Notes to Chapter 2

Epigraph: *A Day When Nothing Is Certain: Writings on the Greek Insurrection*. Web.
1 For discussions of anarchism, violence, and non-violence, see, for example, "Ends and Means," in Peter Marshall, *Demanding the Impossible: A History of Anarchism* (London: Fontana, 1993), 625–38; "Anarchisme, non-violence, quelle synergie?", *Alternatives non violentes*, special issue, 117 (Winter 2000–1); and "Violence, contre violence, non-violence anarchistes," *Réfractions* 5 (Spring 2000).
2 Barbara Epstein, *Political Protest and Cultural Revolution: Nonviolent Direct Action in the 1970s and 1980s* (Berkeley: University of California Press, 1993), 69–81.
3 Roland Breton, "La violence et son contraire dans la libération de l'Inde," *Réfractions* 5 (Spring 2000).
4 Interview in "Toronto: Le Black Bloc passe à l'action," *Casse sociale* 5 (2010): 14.
5 The manual is reproduced and examined in Philip Agee, *Inside the Company: CIA Diary* (London: Penguin, 1975).
6 Oddly, some of those denouncing the "violence" of the Black Blocs offer the fall of the Berlin Wall as a model of non-violent mobilization, as though

shattering a few bank windows was a violent act but not destroying a wall. See, for instance, Dominique Boisvert, "Black Bloc, violence et non-violence," *Presse-toi à gauche!*, May 3, 2012. Web.

7   Gaston Deschênes, "Présentation," in G. Deschênes, *Une capitale éphémère: Montréal et les événements tragiques de 1849* (Montréal: Les Cahiers du Septentrion, 1999).

8   See Mark 11:15–18.

9   See Patrick Tillard, "Une affection bâclée," *Divergences* (August 2006): 3. Web. Our translation. See also Michael Albert, "On trashing and movement building," *Z Magazine* 22, no. 9 (September 2009). Web.

10   Clément Barette, *La pratique de la violence politique par l'émeute: le cas de la violence exercée lors des contre-sommets* (postgraduate thesis, Université de Paris I—Panthéon-Sorbonne, 2002), 90. Our translation.

11   Christos Boukalas, "No One Is Revolutionary Until the Revolution! A Long, Hard Reflection on Athenian Anarchy Through the Prism of a Burning Ban," in *Revolt and Crisis in Greece: Between a Present Yet to Pass and a Future Still to Come*, ed. Antonis Vradis and Dimitris Dalakoglou (Oakland: AK, 2011), 289–94.

12   Boukalas, "No One Is Revolutionary," 279–97.

13   In the brochure "Solidarity with the Anarchist Fighters and All Those Imprisoned for Subversive Actions or Participation in Social Struggles in Greece," ElephantEdition, August 26, 2012.

14   "A Communique on Tactics and Organization to the Black Bloc, from Within the Black Bloc" (2nd ed., July 2001), in *The Black Bloc Papers: An Anthology of Primary Texts from the North American Anarchist Black Bloc 1999–2001* ed. David Van Deusen and Xavier Massot (Oakland: AK, 2002), 198–225. Visit http://www.infoshop.org/amp/bgp/BlackBlockPapers2.pdf.

15   Excerpts from an interview with a member of the *Tute Bianche* who participated in the demonstrations in Prague in 2000, quoted in Amory Starr, "'(Excepting barricades erected to prevent us from peacefully assembling)': So-called 'violence' in the Global North alterglobalization movement," *Social Movement Studies* 5, no. 1 (May 2006): 76.

16   Sian Sullivan, "'We are heartbroken and furious!' Engaging with violence and the (anti-)globalisation movement(s)," *CSGR Working Paper*, 123/03 (2004): 16. Web.

17   "Some Notes on Insurrectionary Anarchism," in *Killing King Abacus* 2. Web.

18   Two companer@s of the Calisse Brigade, "A. Anti. Anti-Capitalista!" June 10, 2007. Web.

19   For a recent overview of the incomplete state of current information, see Steven E. Barkan and Lynne L. Snowden, *Collective Violence* (Boston:

Allyn and Bacon, 2001); and Marco Giugni, "Was it worth the effort? The outcomes and consequences of social movements," *Annual Review of Sociology* 24 (August 1998): 371–93. See also Yves Michaud, *La violence,* 2nd ed. (Paris: Presses Universitaires de France, 1988), 63–64; David E. Apter, "L'apothéose de la violence politique," in *Faut-il s'accommoder de la violence?,* ed. Thomas Ferenczi (Paris: Complexe, 2000), 289; Solomon Lipp, "Reflections on Social and Political Violence," in *Violence and Human Coexistence: Proceedings of the 2nd World Congress of ASEVICO,* vol. 2 (Montreal: Montmorency, 1995), 68, 70; and Jean-Claude Chesnais, *Histoire de la violence* (Paris: Robert Laffont, 1981), 335.

20 Barkan and Snowden, *Collective Violence,* 120.

21 Randall Amster, *Anarchism Today* (Santa Barbara: Praeger, 2012), 147–63.

22 Amster, *Anarchism Today,* 148.

23 For a conclusion reached on the basis of this analytical and political approach, see the section "Un impact politique limité," in Geoffrey Pleyers, "Des Black Blocs aux alter-activistes: pôles et formes d'engagement des jeunes altermondialistes," *Lien social et politiques* 51 (Spring 2004): 130.

24 Frances Fox Piven and Richard A. Cloward, *Poor People's Movements: Why They Succeed, How They Fail* (New York: Vintage, 1979).

25 Ward Churchill, *Pacifism as Pathology: Reflections on the Role of Armed Struggle in North America* (Winnipeg: Arbeiter Ring, 1998), 41–44; Breton, "La violence et son contraire," 77–89.

26 Midge MacKenzie, *Shoulder to Shoulder* (New York: Alfred A. Knopf, 1975), 8–9.

27 Tammy Kovich, "Marching with the Black Bloc—'Violence' and Movement Building," in *Whose Streets? The Toronto G20 and the Challenges of Summit Protest,* ed. Tom Malleson and David Wachsmuth (Toronto: Between the Lines, 2011), 136.

28 On the subject of radical or violent actions and the cycle of reform they can generate, see Chapter 5 in Anders Corr, *No Trespassing: Squatting, Rent Strikes, and Land Struggles Worldwide* (Boston: South End, 1999).

29 Marco Bardesono, "Scontri et fereti al cantiere Tav ...," *Corriere della Serra* (Milan), July 4, 2011, 2. Our translation.

30 Barette, *La pratique de la violence politique,* 97. Our translation.

31 Anonymous, "The Anti-Capitalist March and the Black Bloc," in *Occupy Everything! Anarchists in the Occupy Movement 2009–2011,* ed. Aragorn! (LBC, 2012), 163.

32 Chris Hedges, "The cancer in Occupy," *Truthdig,* February 6, 2012. Web.

33 Brendan Kiley, "May Day anarchists will compensate small businesses whose windows were smashed" in *Slog—The Stranger,* May 3, 2013. Web.

34 *Après avoir tout brûlé...: Suite au Sommet de l'ONTA à Strasbourg en avril 2009 – Correspondance à propos de stratégies et émotions révolutionnaires*, 3. Web.

35 Susie Cagle, "Activists and anarchists speak for themselves at Occupy Oakland," *Truthout*, February 8, 2012. Web.

36 J.A. Myerson, "Interview with Chris Hedges about Black Bloc," *Truthout*, February 9, 2012. Web. For similar comments regarding the meeting of the IMF and the World Bank in Washington in 2000, see Larry Elin, "The Radicalization of Zeke Spier: How the Internet Contributes to Civic Engagement and New Forms of Social Capital," in *Cyberactivism: Online Activism in Theory and Practice*, ed. Martha McCaughey and Michael D. Ayers (London and New York: Routledge, 2003), 105. On the Summit of the Americas in Quebec City (April 2001), see Valérie Dufour, "Les policiers tenus en haleine tout le week-end: les militants repartent satisfaits," *Le Devoir* (Montreal) April 23, 2001, sec. A p. 3.

37 Jean-François Lisée, "Du courier ... en attendant la loi special," *L'Actualité*, May 17, 2012. Web. Our translation.

38 Posted on www.facebook.com/indigne.e.s.valleyfield. Our translation.

39 Kate Evans, "It's Got to Be Silver and Pink: On the Road with Tactical Frivolity," in *We Are Everywhere: The Irresistible Rise of Global Anti-Capitalism*, ed. Notes from Nowhere (London and New York: Verso, 2003), 293; Amory Starr, *Global Revolt: A Guide to the Movements Against Globalization* (London and New York: Zed, 2005), 241; McKay, "DIY Culture: Note Toward an Intro," in *DIY Culture*, ed. McKay, 15.

40 Starr, *Global Revolt*, 244.

41 Evans, "It's Got to Be Silver and Pink," 293; Starr, *Global Revolt*, 219ff.

42 ACME Collective, "N30 Black Bloc communiqué," December 4, 1999. Web.

43 "Les étudiants aux casseurs: 'Nous faisons la loi dans la rue!'" Web. Our translation.

44 Graeme Chester and Ian Welsh, "Rebel of colours: 'Framework' in global social movements," *Sociological Review* (2004): 323ff.

45 Starr, *Global Revolt*, 219.

46 For accounts of these events, see Maxim Fortin, *La résurgence d'une contestation radicale en Amérique du Nord* (M.A. thesis, Université Laval, 2005); Cindy Milstein, "Something did Start in Quebec City: North America's Revolutionary Anticapitalist Movement," in Eddie Yuen, Daniel Burton-Rose, and George Katsiaficas, eds., *Confronting Capitalism: Dispatches From a Global Movement* (New York: Soft Skull, 2004), 126–133; Isabelle Saint-Amand, *Penser la ville close: rue et périmètre de sécurité, Québec 2001* (M.A. thesis, Concordia University, Montreal, 2004); and Félix Thériault-Bérubé, *Les 'Black Blocs' et leur impact sur les autres acteurs du*

mouvement anti-altermondialiste au Québec: le cas du Sommet de Québec en 2001 (M.A. thesis, Université de Montréal, 2006). In the months and years following the CLAC–CASA demonstrations against the Summit of the Americas, Anticapitalist Convergences sprang up in New York, Washington, Chicago, Seattle, Calgary, and elsewhere, adopting the CLAC's principles as found on the Web, including "respect for diversity of tactics."

47   See Christopher Day, "Out now! Toward a strategy of resistance," *Love and Rage* 1, no. 6 (1990): 7.

48   Janet Conway, "Civil resistance and the 'diversity of tactics' in the anti-globalization movement: Problems of violence, silence, and solidarity in activist politics," *Osgoode Hall Law Journal* 41, nos. 2–3 (2003): 519–20. [*Sale* is the French word for "dirty," so a SalAMI is a "dirty friend."—Trans.]

49   Starr, "'(Excepting barricades ...),'" 76.

50   Visit the website of Peoples' Global Action: http://www.nadir.org/nadir/initiativ/agp/en. See also Churchill, *Pacifism as Pathology*.

51   Barette, *La pratique de la violence politique*, 29. Our translation.

52   This critical analysis is presented in Conway, "Civil Resistance."

53   David Van Deusen, "The Emergence of the Black Bloc and the Movement Towards Anarchism," in *The Black Blocs Papers*, ed. David Van Deusen and Xavier Massot (Green Mountain Anarchist Collective) (Baltimore: Black Clover, 2002), 15.

54   BB1, interviewed by the author in Montreal in September 2002, is a 20-year-old male who participated in Black Blocs at the march of May 1, 2000, in Westmount (Quebec); at the demonstrations against the G20 meeting in Montreal in November 2000; against the Summit of the Americas in Quebec City in April 2001; and during the Peoples' Summit in Porto Alegre in the winter of 2001. Our translation.

55   GA10, interview with the author.

56   C. Monnot, "Les altermondialistes ont mobilise massivement en Suisse et en France," *Le Monde*, June 6, 2003.

57   Irène Pereira, "Une sociologie des Black Blocs," *Contretemps*. Web.

58   NumeroZero, "anti-G8 : Communiqué du Houmos Bloc." Web. Our translation.

59   See James C. Scott, *Domination and the Arts of Resistance: Hidden Transcripts* (New Haven: Yale University Press, 1990), 172–82.

60   Scott, *Domination and the Arts of Resistance*, 148.

61   David Graeber, *Direct Action: An Ethnography* (Oakland: AK, 2010), 148.

62   Starr, "'(Excepting barricades ...),'" 72.

63   Martin Pelchat, "Ménard a craint le pire pour les policiers: 'Les Québécois doivent réaliser que la SQ a changé,'" *La Presse* (Montreal), April 28, 2001, sec. B p. 5. Our translation.

64 Including anarchists. See Centre des médias alternatifs du Québec (CMAQ), "Manifeste du Carré noir." Web.
65 According to Paul Hawken, quoted in Karen Goaman, "The Anarchist Travelling Circus: Reflections on Contemporary Anarchism, Anti-Capitalism, and the International Scene," in *Changing Anarchism: Anarchist Theory and Practice in a Global Age*, ed. Jonathan Purkis and James Bowen (Manchester: Manchester University Press, 2004), 172.
66 Author's interview with BB3.
67 Jeffrey Juris, "Violence performed and imagined: Militant action, the Black Bloc and the mass media in Genoa," *Critique of Anthropology* 25, no. 4 (2005): 414–15.
68 Graeber, "The new anarchists," 66.
69 Starr, "'(Excepting barricades…),'" 73.
70 Marc James Léger, "Protesting Degree Zero: On Black Bloc Tactics, Culture, and Building the Movement," in *Protest and Punishment: The Repression of Resistance in the Era of Neoliberal Globalization*, ed. Jeff Shantz (Durham: Carolina Academic Press, 2012), 214–15..
71 Ruth Kinna, *Anarchism* (London: Oneworld, 2005), 202.
72 Tammy Kovich, "The Black Bloc and the New Society," *Upping the Anti* 12 (2011): 17–18.

Notes to Chapter 3

1 I am indebted here to Adreba Solneman, "Du 9 janvier 1978 au 4 novembre 1979," reprinted in *La naissance d'une idée*, vol. 2 (Paris: Belles Émotions, 2002), 56.
2 Seen during the Summit of the Americas in Quebec City, April 2001.
3 Seen during the G8 Summit in Genoa, July 2001.
4 Mario Roy, "À bout de souffle," *La Presse* (Montréal) August 2, 2003, A14. Our translation. Italics added.
5 Clément Barette, *La pratique de la violence politique par l'émeute: le cas de la violence exercée lors des contre-sommets* (M.A. thesis, Université de Paris I—Panthéon-Sorbonne, 2002), 80.
6 See the communiqué "Pourquoi nous étions à Gênes?" in Dupuis-Déri, *Les Black Blocs* (Montréal: Lux, 2003), 181; See also David Graeber, "The new anarchists," *New Left Review* 2, no. 13 (January–February 2002): 66–68 at 65; and Barette, *La pratique de la violence politique*, 79.
7 Amory Starr, Luis Fernandez, and Christian Scholl, eds., *Shutting Down the Streets: Political Violence and Social Control in the Global Era* (New York: NYU Press, 2011), 161–62.

8   Parts of this passage are drawn from my article, "The Black Blocs ten years after Seattle," *Journal for the Study of Radicalism* 4, no. 2 (2010): 45–82.

9   Sian Sullivan, "'We are heartbroken and furious!' Engaging with violence and the (anti-)globalisation movement(s)," CSGR Working Paper 123/03 (2004): 24–26.

10   Sullivan, "We are heartbroken," 30; Francis Dupuis-Déri, "Broyer du noir: Manifestations et répression policière au Québec," *Les ateliers de l'éthique* 1, no. 1 (2006): 58–80.

11   Sullivan, "We are heartbroken," 26.

12   Francis Dupuis-Déri, *Lacrymos: Qu'est-ce qui fait pleurer les anarchistes* (Montréal: Écosociété, 2010).

13   In Sullivan, "We are heartbroken," 30.

14   WOMBLES, "G8 Black Bloc: Report from an activist in Lausanne," 2003.

15   Sian Sullivan, Centre for the Study of Globalisation and Regionalisation, "'Anger is a gift': Or is it? Engaging with violence in the (anti-)globalization movement(s)," *Newsletter* no. 10, September 2003, 1. In this text the author warns against militant violence, which can turn self-destructive or entail collateral damage, including the deaths of non-combatants. A few years later, as discussed elsewhere in this book, a demonstration in Greece turned tragic when three people employed at a bank died of asphyxiation after a Molotov cocktail attack. That said, I do not know if a Black Bloc was responsible. Witnesses mentioned that in the middle of the street, two groups of anarchists involved in the riot debated the idea of torching a bank. For a critical discussion of Greek anarchist groups' responses to the event, see Christos Boukalas, "No One Is Revolutionary Until the Revolution! A Long, Hard Reflection on Athenian Anarchy Through the Prism of a Burning Bank," in *Revolt and Crisis in Greece: Between a Present Yet to Pass and a Future Still to Come*, ed. Antonis Vradis and Dimitris Dalakoglou (Oakland: AK, 2011), 279–97.

16   Two companer@s of the Calisse Brigade, "A. Anti. Anti-Capitalista!" June 10, 2007. Web.

17   George Katsiaficas uses the expression "emotional rationality" in "The Eros Effect," paper presented at the 1989 American Sociological Association National Meetings in San Francisco. Web. See also James Jasper, "L'art de la protestation collective," in *Les formes de l'action collective*, ed. Daniel Cefaï (Paris: Éditions de l'EHESS, 2001), 135–59; and Philippe Braud, *L'émotion en politique* (Paris: Presses de Sciences Po., 1996).

18   Katsiaficas, "The Eros effect," 10; Jasper, "L'art de la protestation collective." See also Braud, *L'émotion en politique*.

19   George E. Marcus, *The Sentimental Citizen Emotion in Democratic Politics* (University Park: Penn State University Press, 2002).

20 Voltairine de Cleyre, *Exquisite Rebel: The Essays of Voltairine de Cleyre—Anarchist, Feminist, Genius*, ed. S. Presley and C. Sartwell (New York: SUNY Press, 2005), 54.

21 Robert Booth and Marc Vallé, "'Black Bloc' anarchists behind anti-cuts rampage reject thuggery claims," *The Guardian* (London), April 1, 2001. Web.

22 Barette, *La violence politique,* 79. Our translation. Italics added.

23 Originally: "Ils [les flics] nous arrêtent pour rien, [...] Faut pas que les flics s'étonnent, / De se faire casser la tête, / C'est normal quand ils nous cognent / Qu'on éprouve de la haine."

24 So, for example, before Bérurier Noir played in Quebec City in June 2004, they had established ties with militant groups such as CLAC, which then set up literature tables at the show with political information in the shape of newspapers, flyers, posters, and the like.

25 Originally: "Marqués par la haine / Les jeunes se déchaînent / On a rien à perdre / Les bagnoles crament / La zone est en flame / Et la folie gagne / Les gamins rebelles / Brûlent des poubelles / Ce soir c'est la fête."

26 Barette, *La violence politique.*

27 Graeber, "The new anarchists," 65.

28 Mike Mowbray, "Blogging the Greek riots: Between aftermath and ongoing engagement," *Resistance Studies* 1 (2012): 10.

29 See "Pourquoi étions-nous à Gênes?"

30 Author's interview with BB1. Our translation.

31 Author's interview with BB2. Our translation.

32 Barette, *La violence politique*, 88. Our translation.

33 Author's interview, conducted in Montreal in March 2002, with GA2, a male activist around 20 years of age, member of an affinity group that sometimes used force and that had been involved in a number of demonstrations in Quebec, including those against the Summit of the Americas in April 2001.

34 Maxim Fortin, "La résurgence d'une contestation radicale en Amérique du Nord" (M.A. thesis, Université Laval, Quebec City, 2005), 103. Our translation.

35 An allusion to Hakim Bey, *TAZ: Zone autonome temporaire*, (Paris: L'éclat, 1998).

36 "Petite carte postale à l'usage des dénonciateurs d'une pseudo-violence du côté manifestant," in *Gênes, 19–20–21 juillet 2001*, ed. Samizdat.net, 199. Our translation.

37 Author's interview, conducted in Strasbourg on June 23, 2003, with AD1, a male activist, 27 years old, who never joined a Black Bloc but who identifies himself as a "communiste libertaire" (anarcho-communist). Took part

in direct actions in Genoa (G8 Summit, July 2001), Brussels (European Summit), and Rome (rally of Kurdish immigrants against the Turkish government's arrest of the Kurd leader Abdullah Ocalan).

38 It is sometimes difficult to sort out to what degree the rise in economic inequality is indeed caused by globalization rather than specifically domestic factors.

39 See, for example, Peter Kropotkin, *The Conquest of Bread* (New York: Dover, [1892]2011.

40 See the note about him in *Dico Rebelle 2004* (Paris: Michalon, 2004).

41 Quoted in the now-defunct Montreal weekly *Mirror*, March 29–April 5, 2001.

42 ACME Collective, "N30 Black Bloc communique," December 4, 1999. Web.

43 Jessa McLean, "In black and running wild," *Toronto Star*, June 27, 2010, A7.

44 Franco Fracassi, *Black Bloc: Viaggio nel pianeta nero* (Lecco: Studio, 2011), 10–11. Also, on page 26, the author cites a German activist who stresses the same point. Thanks to David Pulizzotto for the translation.

45 *Manifeste du Carré noir* (Montreal: Centre des médias alternatifs du Québec, 2012). Web. Our translation.

46 J.A. Myerson, "Interview with Chris Hedges about Black Bloc," *Truthout*, February 9, 2012. Web.

47 Fortin, *La résurgence*, 105. Our translation.

48 Nicolas Tavaglione, "Qui a peur de l'homme noir?", *Le Courrier* (Geneva), June 11, 2003, 4. Our translation.

49 Barette, *La violence politique*, 92. Our translation.

50 Barette, *La violence politique*, 80. Our translation.

51 Jean-Jacques Rousseau, *The Social Contract*, trans. Maurice Cranston (London: Penguin, 1968), 141.

52 Voltairine de Cleyre, *The Voltairine De Cleyre Reader*, ed. A.J. Brigati (Oakland: AK, 2004), 59.

53 Barette, *La violence politique*, 53. Our translation.

54 Barette, *La violence politique*, 89. Our translation.

55 Author's interview with BB2. Our translation.

56 Tavaglione, "Qui a peur de l'homme noir?", 4. Our translation.

57 Herbert Marcuse, *An Essay on Liberation* (Boston: Beacon, 1971) 66–67; "The Problem of Violence and Radical Opposition," in Herbert Marcuse, *The New Left and the 1960s: Collected Papers,* vol. III (New York: Routledge, 2005), 62; Hannah Arendt, *Crises of the Republic: Lying in Politics, Civil Disobedience, On Violence, Thoughts on Politics and Revolution* (New York: Houghton Mifflin Harcourt, 1972), 51–101; Mario Turchetti, *Tyrannie et tyrannicide de l'Antiquité à nos jours* (Paris: Presses Universitaires de France, 2001).

Notes to Chapter 4

1. As one old time French Black Blocker said in a letter, after the NATO Summit in Strasbourg, in 2009 (*Après avoir tout brûlé... : Suite au Sommet de l'OTAN à Strasbourg en avril 2009 – Correspondance à propos de stratégies et émotions révolutionnaires*, p. 4. Web). Our translation.

2. BB2. Our translation.

3. BB1. Our translation.

4. Clément Barette, *La pratique de la violence politique par l'émeute: le cas de la violence exercée lors des contre-sommets* (M.A. thesis, Université de Paris I—Panthéon-Sorbonne, 2002), 105. Our translation.

5. Barette, *La pratique de la violence politique,* 105.

6. Barette, *La pratique de la violence politique,* 76.

7. BB9, a male anarchist in his mid-30s, interviewed in Paris in 2013.

8. Nicolas (Barricada Collective), "The Black Bloc in Quebec: An Analysis," in *The Black Blocs Papers,* ed. David Van Deusen and Xavier Massot (Green Mountain Anarchist Collective) (Baltimore: Black Clover, 2002), 193. Our translation.

9. Tillard, "Une affection bâclée," *Divergences* (August 2006). Web.

10. Randall Amster, *Anarchism Today* (Santa Barbara: Praeger, 2012), 32–33.

11. In Amory Starr, Luis Fernandez, and Christian Scholl, eds., *Shutting Down the Streets: Political Violence and Social Control in the Global Era* (New York: NYU Press, 2011), 156.

12. In "The civil rights movement and the Black Bloc," he had this to say about the events surrounding the Toronto G20 Summit: "Nothing in the lives of a single oppressed person anywhere in the world changes as a result and the humdrum nightmare of global capitalism goes on unaltered. No amount of situationist verbiage can alter that fact." *Upping the Anti*, Web.

13. Naggh, *Nouvelles de l'assemblée générale du genre humain* (Paris: Belles émotions, 2004), 27–28.

14. Van Deusen and Massot, eds., *The Black Bloc Papers*, 10.

15. See "Pourquoi étions-nous à Gênes?" in Dupuis-Déri, *Les Black Blocs* (Montréal: Lux, 2003); Francis Dupuis-Déri, "En deuil de révolution?", *Réfractions* 13 (2004).

16. Dupuis-Déri, "En deuil de révolution?"

17. Author's interview with BB3. Our translation.

18. Author's interview with AD1. Our translation.

19. Andy Chan, "Anarchists, violence and social change: Perspectives from today's grassroots," *Anarchist Studies* 3, no. 1 (1995): 54–56.

20 Edward Avery-Natale, "'We're here, we're queer, we're anarchists': The nature of identification and subjectivity among Black Blocs," *Anarchist Development in Cultural Studies* 1 (2010): 95. See also A.K. Thompson, *Black Bloc White Riot: Anti-Globalization and the Genealogy of Dissent* (Oakland: AK, 2010),124.

21 Thompson, *Black Bloc White Riot:* Chapter 4, "You Can't Do Gender in a Riot."

22 Mary Black, "Letter from inside the Black Bloc," June 24, 2001. Web.

23 Krystalline Kraus, "Sisters in struggle," *rabble.ca*, June 21, 2002. Web.

24 On the subject of militant violence and machismo, see Robin Morgan, *The Demon Lover* (New York: W.W. Norton, 1989); and Lee Quinby, "Taking the Millennialist Pulse of Empire's Multitude: A Genealogical Feminist Diagnosis," in *Empire's New Clothes: Reading Hardt and Negri,* ed. Paul A. Passavant and Jodi Dean (London: Routledge, 2004), 236–42.

25 Rachel Neumann, "A place for rage," in *The Battle of Seattle: The New Challenge to Capitalist Globalization,* ed. Eddie Yuen, Daniel Burton Rose, and George Katsiaficas (New York: Soft Skull, 2001), 111.

26 I am indebted here to Émeline Fourment, who is currently a postgraduate student at l'Institut de science politique in Paris and is writing a thesis on the influence of feminist ideas on the practice and discourse of the radical left in Göttingen, Germany, and to Aurélie Audeval, a doctoral candidate at l'École des hautes études en sciences sociales in Paris, who lived in Germany for a long time and wrote a thesis on Spartakist women.

27 Black Women Movement, "Women in the Black Bloc." Web. See also an interview with an American man who asserts there is no difference between men and women in the Black Blocs. In Franco Fracassi, *Black Bloc: Viaggio nel pianeta nero* (Italie: Alpine Studio, 2011), 23.

28 See, for example, John Bohstedt, "The Myth of the Feminine Food Riot: Women as Proto-Citizens in English Community Politics, 1790–1810," in *Women and Politics in the Age of the Democratic Revolution,* ed. Harriet B. Applewhite and Darline G. Levy (Ann Arbor: University of Michigan Press, 1990) 21–61; Ann Hansen, *Direct Action: Memoirs of an Urban Guerrilla* (Toronto: Between the Lines, 2002), 487–93; and "Interview with Rote Zora," in Dark Star, ed., *Quiet Rumours: An Anarcha-Feminist Reader* (Oakland: AK, 2012), 115–19.

29 Maggie, Rayna, Michael, Matt (The Rock Bloc Collective), "Stick it to the Manarchy." Web.

30 BB8, a 23-year-old woman whose involvement in the antiwar movement began at age 15. Interviewed in Montreal in 2013.

31 Author's interview with BB3. Our translation.

32 Author's interview with BB3. Our translation.

33   My estimates may have been overly precise in Francis Dupuis-Déri, "Black Blocs: bas les masques," *Mouvements* 25 (January–February 2003): 76. See "Pourquoi étions-nous à Gênes?", 180–8. Web. See also Black, "Letter from inside the Black Bloc." In the case of a Black Bloc of 40 individuals at the G8 meeting in Deauville, France, in June 2011, a journalist from the magazine *L'Express* who had infiltrated the group counted "five girls, followers rather than leaders" (our translation). See Antoine Marnet, "Black blocs: plongée dans l'ultragauche anti-G8," *L'Express*, June 5, 2011. Web.

34   "Pourquoi étions-nous à Gênes?"

35   Shawn, "Don't forget the Minute 'Women'!" in Van Deusen and Massot, *The Black Bloc Papers*, 80.

36   Starr, Fernandez, and Scholl, *Shutting Down the Streets*, 160.

37   Interview with BB7. Our translation.

38   Interview with BB8. Our translation.

39   *Après avoir tout brûlé …: Suite au Sommet de l'OTAN à Strasbourg en avril 2009—Correspondance à propos de stratégies et émotions révolutionnaires,* 8, 9–10. Web. Our translation.

40   Sian Sullivan, "'Anger is a gift': Or is it? Engaging with violence in the (anti-)globalization movement(s)," *Newsletter of the Centre for the Study of Globalisation and Regionalisation*, no. 10 (September 2003): 12.

41   T-Bone Kneegrabber, "Real feminists don't get raped and other fairy tales," *The Peak*, Special Issue: "Sexual Assault in Activist Communities" (2002): 38–39.

42   Kneegrabber, "Real feminists don't get raped."

43   Mark LeVine, "The revolution, back in black," *Aljazeera*, February 2, 2013. Web.

44   Toronto Police, *G20 Summit Toronto, Ontario June 2010—Toronto Police Service After-Action Review* (June 2011), 2.

45   Letter signed by Louise Arsenault, *Journal de Montréal*, February 26, 2013, 23.

46   Dave Abel et al., "Organized anarchy," *Toronto Sun*, June 27, 2010, 5.

47   David Akin, "Need for 'common action,'" *Toronto Sun*, June 27, 2010, 8. Italics added.

48   *Toronto Star*, June 28, 2010, A2.

49   Garlan, "Sommet du G8: Les Huit." Our translation. Italics added.

50   "Un mort à Gênes: martyr ou dégénération d'une cause juste," AFP-Presse espagnole (Madrid), July 21, 2001. Our translation.

51   Rick Anderson, "The anarchists of nostalgia," *Seattle Weekly*, May 2, 2012. Web.

52   David Horsey, "Today's anarchists are just brats in black," *Los Angeles Times*, May 22, 2012. Web.

53 Laurent Zecchini, "Les 'antimondialistes' sabotent le Sommet de Göteborg," *Le Monde*, June 17–18, 2001. In a similar vein, see Christian Spillman, "Reprise des affrontements à Gênes, journée rouge pour le G8," AFP, July 21, 2001, and André Pratte, "Les alter-hypocrites," *La Presse*, July 31, 2003, A9.

54 France 2 news report, July 21, 2001. Our translation.

55 Quoted by Christian Losson and Paul Quinio, *Génération Seattle: les rebelles de la mondialisation* (Paris: Grasset, 2002), 156. Our translation. Italics added.

56 Losson and Quinio, *Génération Seattle*, 166. Our translation.

57 Losson, "Des antimondialistes dans la tactique de l'affrontement," *Libération*, June 18, 2001. Web. Our translation.

58 Harvey Molotch, "Media and Movements," in *The Dynamics of Social Movements*, ed. Mayer N. Zald and John D. McCarthy (Cambridge, M.A.: Winthrop, 1979), 81.

59 Referring to a demonstration at a French–Italian border crossing prior to the G8 Summit in Genoa, a journalist depicted it as "a rather good-natured demonstration" (TF1 televised news report, July 14, 2001). The same expression—"bon enfant"—and tone were used the next day on the France 2 TV channel. And the June 2, 2003, edition of *La Tribune de la Genève* ran a report titled "A good-natured demonstration" regarding a non-violent march against the G8 Summit in Genoa. All translations here are ours.

60 Nathan Hervé, "L'Europe sociale sur la Promenade," *Libération*, December 7, 2000. Our translation.

61 Yves Michaud, *La violence*, 2nd ed. (Paris: Presses Universitaires de France, 1988), 48–52.

62 Excerpt from an interview with three women who joined Black Blocs during the Quebec student strike in 2012. The interview was conducted by Boris Proulx for his radio news feature, "Au coeur du Black Bloc: entrevue exclusive avec trois militants radicales" (Inside the Black Bloc: An exclusive interview with three radical activists), CIBL (Montreal), May 25, 2012. Web. Our translation. A British activist expressed a similar outlook in an interview quoted in Fracassi, *Black Bloc*, 33.

63 See the very interesting text by Gadi Wolfsfed, "Media, protest, and political violence: A transactional analysis," *Journalism Monographs* 127 (June 1991); see also Amitai Etzioni, *Demonstration Democracy* (New York: Gordon and Breach, 1970); and William A. Gamson, *The Strategy of Social Protest* (Homewood: Dorsey, 1975), Chapter 6.

64 Chris Samuel, "Throwing bricks at the brick wall: The G20 and the antinomies of protest," *Studies in Political Economy* 90 (2012): 18–20.

65 Robert Booth and Marc Vallé, "'Black Bloc' anarchists behind anti-cuts rampage reject thuggery claims," *The Guardian* (London), April 1, 2001. Web.

66 Author's e-mail interview, January 2004, with a 36-year-old woman who had participated in Black Blocs and was politically active mainly in New York and Toronto. Our translation.

67 Mario Roy, "À bout de souffle," *La Presse* (Montréal) August 2, 2003, A14.

68 Lynn Owens and L. Kendall Palmer, "Making the news: Anarchist counter-public relations on the World Wide Web," *Critical Studies in Media Communication* 20, no. 4 (2003): 335–61.

69 Yves Boisvert, "Je suis un casseur," *La Presse* (Montréal), May 12, 2012. Web.

70 Starhawk, *Webs of Power*, 122–23 (Randall Amster, *Anarchism Today*, 32).

71 Donatella della Porta and Sidney Tarrow, "After Genoa and New York: The antiglobal movement, the police, and terrorism," Social Science Research Council (Winter 2001). Web.

72 Olivier Fillieule and Jean-Pierre Masse, "Peur sur la ville: les inflexions de la doctrine et de la pratique du maintien de l'ordre sous l'effet du développement des mobilisations altermondialistes," paper delivered at the conference on "Policing Political Protest After Seattle," Fiskebackekil, Sweden, May 1–5, 2004.

73 Christophe Aguiton, "Quelques éléments pour la discussion après Gênes," in Samizadt.net, *Gênes 19–20–21 juillet 2001: Multitudes en marche contre l'empire* (Paris: Reflex, 2002), 267.

74 Susan George, "G8: Are you happy?", *CorpWatch*, June 24, 2001. Web.

75 Léonce Aguirre, "'Black Bloc,' violences et intoxication," *Rouge*, June 5, 2003. Our translation. Italics added.

76 Political Matti, "The Summit protests: A dissenting view," *Black Flag* 225, 5; Aufheben, "L'anticapitalisme comme idéologie ... et comme movement" (2002). Web.

77 Alex Trocchi, "For the Insurrection to Succeed, We Must First Destroy Ourselves," in *Revolt and Crisis in Greece: Between a Present Yet to Pass and a Future Still to Come,* ed. Vradis and Dalakoglou (Oakland and London: AK and Occupied London, 2011), 313–14.

78 Sasha K, "Some notes on insurrectionary anarchism," *Killing King Abacus* 2 (July 8, 2001). Web.

79 Autonomous University Collective, "Who Is the Black Bloc? Where Is the Black Bloc?", in *Springtime: The New Student Rebellions,* ed. Clare Solomon and Tania Palmieri (London: Verso, 2011), 130.

80 Anonymous, "En défense des rebelles de Seattle ou comment nourrir son anarchiste intérieur," *Les temps modernes* 607 (2000): 220–56. Our translation.

81 Alexander Cockburn, "So who did win in Seattle? Liberals rewrite history." Web.

82 "CUPE supports protests at wall," April 18, 2001. Web.

83 As told to the author in June 2013. See also Jeff Shantz, "Unions, Direct Action, and the G20 Protests," in *Whose Streets? The Toronto G20 and the Challenges of Summit Protest*, ed. Tom Malleson and David Wachsmuth (Toronto: Between the Lines, 2011), 60; Clarice Kuhling, "Forms of Protest Reflect Our Power: Radical Strategy and Mass Mobilizations," also in *Whose Streets,* 169.

84 "Les pays pauvres demeurent en plan, déplore Oxfam-Québec," *Le Journal de Montréal*, July 31, 2003, 3. Our translation.

85 The speech was captured on video and can be viewed at www.dailymotion.com/video/xjtkam_fiaccolata-no-tav-a-torino-intervento-di-alberto-perino_news#.UcYs9BZECWc, at 1:35 min. See also Cristina Bangau, *We Are All Black Block! The NOTAV Protest Movement and Geographies of Intervention* (M.A. thesis, Department of Sociology and Social Anthropology, Central European University, Budapest, 2013).

86 See "Pourquoi nous étions à Gênes," 178.

87 Tom Turner and Judith Barish, "Environmental, labor leaders condemn violence," *World Trade Observer*, Seattle, 1999. Web.

88 Susan George, *Un autre monde est possible si . . .* (Paris: Fayard, 2004) 267. Our translation. Italics added.

89 George, *Un autre monde,* 262. Our translation.

90 George, *Un autre monde,* 263. Our translation.

91 Founder and leader of the Trotskyite party Ligue communiste révolutionnaire (LCR).

92 Author's interview with V10, conducted in Paris on December 11, 2003. Our translation. This 24-year-old man carried out direct actions—destruction of property and pillage—in Nice (December 2000), Genoa (July 2001), and Annemasse (June 2003), and took part in the camp at the Village alternatif anticapitalist et anti-guerre (VAAAG) during the 2003 G8 Summit.

93 "The first embedded protest," *The Guardian*, June 18, 2005 (quoted in Paul Hewson, "'It's the Politics, Stupid': How Neoliberals, NGO's, and Rock Stars Hijacked the Global Justice Movement at Glenneagles . . . and How We Let Them," in David Harvie et al., eds., *Shut Them Down! The G8, Gleneagles 2005 and the Movement of Movements* (West Yorkshire and New York: Dissent! G8 and Autonomedia, 2005), 135.

94 "Ure urges anarchists to 'go home,'" *Edinburgh Evening News*, July 5, 2005 (quoted in Hewson, "It's the Politics, Stupid," 149).

95 Author's interview conducted in Montreal in March 2002 with GA1, a man about 20 years of age, whose affinity group sometimes used force and who

participated in a number of demonstrations in Quebec, including the one against the Summit of the Americas in April 2001. Our translation.

96 Christian Spillmann, "Gênes: violences, discorde, les dirigeants du G8 n'ont pas de quoi pavoiser," AFP, July 22, 2001. Our translation.

97 Dominique Von Burg, "La casse ne doit pas devenir fatale," *La Tribune de Genève*, June 2, 2003, p. 1. Our translation. Italics added.

98 Aguiton, "Quelques éléments," 265. Our translation. Italics added.

99 Statement made at a press conference and included in "La répression atteint un sommet à Québec," a special radio report by Alain Chénier and France Émond, CIBL (Montreal), April 23, 2001, and in the film *Zones grises*, by David Nadeau and Nicolas Bélanger (Québec: Hobogays et Paysdenvie Productions, 2002). Our translation.

100 Kolonel Klepto and Major Up Evil, "The Clandestine Insurgent Rebel Clown Army Goes to Scotland via a Few Other Places," in *Shut Them Down!*.

101 Analysts of social movements have elucidated the dynamic whereby political actors strive to appear respectable in the eyes of the state. According to Doug McAdam, Sidney Tarrow, and Charles Tilly, every "official political regime implicitly draws up a list of political actors who have the right to exist, formulate demands, and routinely obtain resources controlled by the government." *Dynamics of Contention* (Cambridge: Cambridge University Press, 2001), 146–47. Our translation. See also Félix Thériault-Bérubé, "Les 'Black Blocs' et leur impact sur les autres acteurs du mouvement anti-altermondialiste au Québec: le cas du Sommet de Québec en 2001" (M.A. thesis, Université de Montréal, 2006), 89.

102 Michaud, *La violence*, 65. Our translation.

103 Michel Barillon, *ATTAC, encore un effort pour réguler la mondialisation!* (Castelnau-le-Lez: Climats, 2001).

104 Olivier Fillieule, *Stratégies de la rue: les manifestations en France* (Paris: Presses de Science po, 1997), 273. Our translation.

105 Isabelle Sommier, "Paradoxes de la contestation: la contribution des services d'ordre syndicaux à la pacification des conflits sociaux," in *Violence and Human Existence: Proceedings of the Second World Congress of l'ASEVICO* (Montreal: Montmorency, 1995), 333. Our translation. See also Dominique Cardon and Jean-Philippe Heurtin, "Tenir les rangs. Les services d'encadrement des manifestations ouvrières (1909–1936)," in *La manifestation*, ed. Pierre Favre (Paris: Presses de la fondation nationale des sciences politiques, 1990), 123–55.

106 Quotations are drawn from Losson and Quinio, *Génération Seattle*, 167. All translations are ours.

107 George, *Un autre monde est possible si*, 270. Our translation.

108 Sid Ryan, "Thousands stood up for humanity," *Toronto Star*, June 29, 2010. Web.

109 Samuel, "Throwing bricks at the brick wall," 22.

110 Judy Rebick, "Breaking windows is not a revolutionary act," *rabble.ca*, February 16, 2010. Web.

111 Judy Rebick, "Toronto is burning! Or is it?" *rabble.ca*, June 27, 2010. Web.

112 Moisés Naím, "Lori's war," *Foreign Policy* (Spring 2000): 49.

113 Quoted by Timothy Egan, "Talks and Turmoil: The Violence," *New York Times*, December 2, 1999, A1. In an article published later, "Window-smashing hurt our cause," she claims to have been misquoted but nevertheless criticizes the anarchists' use of force.

114 "The Geneva Business Dialogue," *Corporate Europe Observer*, no. 2 (October 1998). Web.

115 Isabelle Saint-Amand, "Penser la ville close: rue et périmètre de sécurité, Québec 2001" (M.A. thesis, Concordia University, Montreal, 2004). Our translation.

116 Quoted by Éric Budry, "Les altermondialistes refusent le piège des groupuscules violents," *La Tribune de Genève*, June 2, 2003, 3. Our translation.

117 Quoted in Losson and Quinio, *Génération Seattle*, 167. Our translation.

118 Quoted in Thériault-Bérubé, *Les "Black Blocs" et leur impact*, 110. Our translation.

119 Quoted in *Le Journal de Montréal*, April 22, 2001. Our translation.

120 "Conférence de presse du premier ministre, M. Bernard Landry, sur le bilan du Sommet des Amériques et du Sommet des peuples," Quebec City, April 23, 2001. Our translation.

121 Quoted in Christine Courcol and Stéphanie Pertuiset, "Une grande marche pacifique d'un côté, une poignée d'extrémistes de l'autre," AFP, April 22, 2001. Our translation.

122 Stéphane Batigne, "J'ai joué le jeu de la manifestation," *Le Devoir* (Montréal), April 24, 2001. Our translation.

Notes to Conclusion

The following section draws on material included in Francis Dupuis-Déri, ed., *À qui la rue? Répression policière et mouvements sociaux* (Montréal: Écosociété, 2013).

1 Toronto Police Service, After-Action Review, *G20 Summit—Toronto, Ontario—June 2010* (Toronto: June 2011), 11–13.

2 TPS After-Action Review, *G20 Summit*, 13.

3 TPS After-Action Review, *G20 Summit*, 13.

4   The problem was not altogether new, having already arisen at the May Day rally in New York in 2000. See David Van Deusen and Xavier Massot, eds., *The Black Blocs Papers* (Green Mountain Anarchist Collective) (Baltimore: Black Clover, 2002), 81.

5   See Lyn Gerry, "Linguistic analysis of the Black Bloc communiqué: Refutation of the claims that the N30 Black Bloc communiqué is 'proof' that they are agents provocateurs" [first published on http://www.infosho.org, but no longer posted). See also "Gênes: police infiltrée par le Black Bloc ou le contraire." Web.

6   Susan George and Martin Wolf, *La Mondialisation libérale* (Paris: Bernard Grasset-Les Échos, 2002), 166. Our translation. Italics added.

7   Murray Dobbin, "Is this what a police state looks like?", *rabble.ca*, June 30, 2010. Web. Italics added.

8   Franco Fracassi, *Black Bloc: Viaggio nel pianeta nero* (Lecco: Studio, 2011), 81–82.

9   Fracassi, *Black Bloc*, 136.

10 Agence France Presse, "G20 de Cannes: opération anti "black blocks" à la frontière franco-italienne," *Le Point*, October 28, 2011. Web.

11 "Les altermondialistes défilent à Nice contre le G20," *Le Figaro*, November 1, 2011. Web.

12 Haroon Siddique, "G8 summit protest: riot police arrest 57 in raid of London HQ," *The Guardian*, June 12, 2013. Web.

13 Donatella della Porta and Lorenzo Zamponi, "Protest and policing on October 15th, global day of action: The Italian case," *Policing and Society* 23, no. 1 (2013): 67.

14 Gerry McNeilly, *Policing the Right to Protest: G20 Systemic Review Report*, Toronto, Office of the Independent Police Review Director, 2012, v.

15 McNeilly, *Policing the Right to Protest*, v, ix.

16 TPS, *G20 Summit*. See also Ombudsman Ontario, "Caught in the Act: Investigation into the Ministry of Community Safety and Correctional Services, Conduct in Relation to Ontario Regulation 233/10 under the Public Works Protection Act," Toronto, December 2010. Web. See also Organization of American States, International Commission of Human Rights, "Document en soutien à l'audience générale portant sur la situation des libertés d'expression, de réunion et d'association au Canada, de même que le droit à la liberté, à la sécurité et à l'intégrité de la personne," Washington, October 25, 2010. Web.

17 Rob Evans and Paul Lewis, "Political activists sue MET over relationship with police spies," *The Guardian*, November 21, 2012. Web. See also Amelia Hill, "Former spy Mark Kennedy sues police for 'failing to stop him falling in love,'" *The Guardian*, November 25, 2012. Web.

18   Her Majesty's Inspectorate of Constabulary (HMIC), *A Review of National Police Units Which Provide Intelligence on Criminality Associated with Protest* (London: HMIC, 2012), 26. Web.

19   Camille Polloni, "Mark Kennedy: la taupe de Tarnac," *Les Inrockuptibles*, March 13, 2012. Web.

20   Pierre Hazan, "À Genève, fureur autour des policiers-casseurs: visages masqués, ils ont pénétré dans un des lieux de la contestation et s'en sont pris à des non-violents," *Libération*, June 3, 2003.

21   Brian Myles, "Agents de la SQ pris en 'flagrant délit,'" *Le Devoir* (Montréal), March 14, 2009.

22   Author's interview with BB2. On the subject of police infiltrators, agents provocateurs, and police tactics, see Olivier Fillieule, *Stratégies de la rue: les manifestations en France* (Paris: Presses de Sciences Po., 1997), 340–52; J.-P. Brunet, *La police de l'ombre: indicateurs et provocateurs dans la France contemporaine* (Paris: Seuil, 1990); G.T. Marx, "Thoughts on a neglected category of social movement participant: The agent provocateur and the informant," *American Journal of Sociology* 80 (1974): 404–29; Victor Serge, *Ce que tout révolutionnaire doit savoir de la repression* (Paris: Maspero, [1925]1977), 9–32; and a very revealing interview with a police agent who infiltrated the "autonomous" circles in Europe, in *Le Nouvel Observateur*, January 24, 1983.

23   Victor Serge, "Agents provocateurs," reprinted in Serge, *Le Rétif: Articles parus dans "L'Anarchie" 1909–1912*, ed. Yves Pagès (Paris: Librairie Monnier, 1989), 209–10. Our translation.

24   During the demonstrations in Thessaloniki against the EU Summit in June 2003, communist militants also spread the rumour that anarchists were agents of the state. See "What I do for a living ... or how I came to be a victim of Molotov cocktail friendly fire and lived to tell the tale," *Rolling Thunder* 1 (2005): 52.

25   An issue discussed in Ruth Kinna, *Anarchism* (Oxford: Oneworld, 2005), 204.

26   Dupuis-Déri, *À qui la rue?*

27   See *Berlusconi's Mousetrap*, dir. Eamonn Crudden, prod. Indymedia.ie (2002). The film can viewed at http://vimeo.com/8672001.

28   Patrick F. Gillham and Gary T. Marx, "Complexity and irony in policing and protesting: The World Trade Organization in Seattle," *Social Justice* 27, no. 2 (2000): 212–36.

29   Karen Pearlston, "APEC Days at UBC: Student Protests and National Security in an Era of Trade Liberation," in *Whose National Security? Canadian State Surveillance and the Creation of Enemies,* ed. Gary Kinsman, Dieter K. Buse, and Mercedes Steedman (Toronto: Between the Lines, 2000), 268.

30   J.A. Frank, "La dynamique des manifestations violentes," *Revue canadienne de science politique* 17, no. 2 (June 1984): 325–49.

31   Dupuis-Déri, *À qui la rue?*

32   Other studies have brought to light the importance of examining police repression on the local and municipal levels. See Alex S. Vitale, "The command and control and Miami models at the 2004 Republican National Convention: New forms of policing protests," *Mobilization* 12, no. 4 (2007): 403–15; and David Waddington and Mike King, "The impact of the local: Police public-order strategies during the G8 Justice and home affairs ministerial meetings," *Mobilization* 12, no. 4 (2007): 417–30.

33   Patrick Rafail, "Asymmetry in Protest Control? Comparing Protest Policing in Montreal, Toronto, and Vancouver," *Mobilization* 15, no. 4 (2010): 489–509. See also Frank, "La dynamique des manifestations violentes."

34   Randy Borum and Chuck Tilby, "Anarchist direct actions: A challenge for law enforcement," *Studies in Conflict and Terrorism* 28 (2005): 201–23.

35   Luis A. Fernandez, *Policing Dissent: Social Control and the Anti-Globalization Movement* (New Brunswick: Rutgers University Press, 2008), 156ff; Michael Rosie and Hugo Gorringe, "'The anarchists' World Cup': Respectable protest and media panics," *Social Movement Studies* 8, no. 1 (2009): 35–53.

36   In Fernandez, *Policing Dissent*, 158.

37   Chris Greenwood, "Black Bloc: Name of the sinister group plotting to sabotage Baroness Thatcher's funeral with 're-enactment' of poll-tax riots,'" *Mail Online*, April 11, 2013. Web.

38   Integrated Security Unit Joint Intelligence Group, 2010 G8 Summit, *Intelligence Report*, June 3, 2009, 6–7.

39   For additional references to anarchism, this time in a document of the Canadian Security Intelligence Service (CSIS), see *Report No. 2000/08: Anti-Globalization—A Spreading Phenomenon*. Web.

40   Jeffrey Monaghan and Kevin Walby, "'They attacked the city': Security intelligence, the sociology of protest policing, and the anarchist threat at the 2010 Toronto G20 summit," *Current Sociology* 60, no. 5 (2012): 658. See also Monaghan and Walby, "Making up 'terror identities': Security intelligence, Canada's integrated threat assessment center, and social movement suppression," *Policing and Society* 22, no. 2 (2012): 133–51.

41   Monaghan and Walby, "'They attacked the city,'" 662.

42   Monaghan and Walby, "'They attacked the city,'" 658.

43   Monaghan and Walby, "'They attacked the city,'" 664.

44   *Le Figaro*, September 14, 2001, 20, quoted in "Haro sur l'ennemi intérieur: 'l'antimondialisme'," August 23, 2002. Web.

45 Giorgio Agamben and Yildune Lévy, "Le secret le mieux gardé de l'affaire de Tarnac," *Le Monde*, November 15, 2012, 29. Our translation.

46 As an amusing sidelight to this incident, among the 5,000 books belonging to one of the apprehended *anarcho-autonomes*, 27 were deemed of interest by the investigators, including *Les Black Blocs*! See Gaël Cogne, "Les livres de Coupat sur PV," *Libération*, April 21, 2009. Web.

47 Marc Thibodeau, "Ce sera le procès de l'antiterrorisme français," *La Presse*, November 10, 2012, A26.

48 Olivier Cahn, "La répression des 'black blocs,' prétexte à la domestication de la rue protestataire," *Archives de politique criminelle* 32 (2010): 168. Our translation.

49 Antoine Roger, "Syndicalistes et poseurs de bombes: Modalités du recours à la violence dans la construction des 'intérêts' vitivinicoles' languedociens," *Cultures et Conflits* 81–82 (2011).

50 *Le Figaro*, September 14, 2001, 20, quoted in "Haro sur l'ennemi intérieur." Our translation.

51 Cahn, "La répression des 'black blocs.'"

52 *EU Definition of Terrorism: Anarchists to Be Targeted as (Terrorists) Alongside al Qaida*, State Watch analysis no. 10, visit database.statewatch. org/article.asp?aid=6385.

53 Louis J. Freeh, *Threat of Terrorism to the United States*, report submitted to the Senate Select Committee on Intelligence, May 10, 2001; Dale L. Watson, *Threat of Terrorism to the United States*, report submitted to the Senate Select Committee on Intelligence, April 6, 2002.

54 Council of the European Union, Note 5712/02 ENFOPOL 18, January 29, 2002. Visit http://www.statewatch.org/news/2002/feb/05712.pdf. Italics added. Note that to forestall any ambiguity the Working Party furthermore defined such acts as infractions to the first article of the "Council Framework Decision on combating terrorism." Visit http://eur-lex.europa.eu/LexUriServ/LexUriServ.do?uri=CELEX:32002F0475:FR:HTML.

55 Francesco Alberti, "Maroni: in Val di Susa tentato omicidio," *Courriere Della Serra*, July 5, 2011, 1. Our translation.

56 Quoted in "Haro sur l'ennemi intérieur." Our translation.

57 Michelle Malkin, "Invasion of the anarchists: The 'anti-capitalist convergence,'" *Capitalism Magazine,* February 2002. Web.

58 *Figaro Magazine*, October 6, 2001. Our translation.

59 On the media coverage of demonstrations, see Andrea M. Langlois, "Mediating transgressions: The global justice movement and Canadian news media," Master's thesis, Concordia University, Montreal, 2004. Regarding the equation of protestors' "violence" with that of radical Islamists, see Leo

Panitch, "Violence as a tool of order and change: The war on terrorism and the anti-globalization movement," *Monthly Review* 54, no. 2 (2002). Web.

60 Tim Dunne, "Anarchistes et Al-Qaeda," *La Presse*, July 8, 2005, A23. Our translation. For other sources of this kind of discourse, see Dupuis-Déri, "Broyer du noir: Manifestations et repression policière au Québec," *Les ateliers de l'éthique* 1, no. 1 (2006): 58–80. Web. See also an updated version in Dupuis-Déri, ed., *À qui la rue?*

61 "Black Bloc anarchists emerge," BBC, February 1, 2013. Web.

62 Donatella della Porta and Sidney Tarrow, "After Genoa and New York: The antiglobal movement, the police, and terrorism," *Social Science Research Council* (Winter 2001). Web. See also *Berlusconi's Mousetrap*.

63 TPS After-Action Review, *G20 Summit*, 62.

64 See the July 6, 2011, issues of *Corriere della Serra,* 19, and *Repubblica,* 18.

65 For a good example of this police tactic, see the photo accompanying the article by Raymond Gervais and Sébastien Rodrigue, "Manifestation antimondialisation: la police exhibe le matériel saisi hier," *La Presse*, April 28, 2002.

66 Jill Mahoney, "'Weapons' seized in G20 arrests not what they seem," *Globe and Mail* (Toronto), June 29, 2010. Web.

67 David Graeber, "On the phenomenology of giant puppets: Broken Windows, Imaginary Jars of Urine, and the Cosmological Role of the Police in American Culture," in Graeber, *Possibilities: Essays on Hierarchy, Rebellion, and Desire* (Oakland: AK, 2007), 388–89.

68 Visit http://www.wdm.org.uk.

69 See the photo in the *Toronto Star*, July 1, 2010, GT2.

70 Mawashi, "Law Enforcement." Web.

71 Visit http://www.policeordnance.com. Note that the passages referred to no longer appear on the company's website.

72 Daniel Dylan Young, "Autonomia and the Origin of the Black Bloc." Web.

73 Autonomous University Collective, "Who is the Black Bloc? Where is the Black Bloc?", in *Springtime: The New Student Rebellions,* ed. Clare Solomon and Tania Palmieri (London: Verso, 2011), 130.

FURTHER READINGS

In cyberspace, there are plenty of communiqués, letters, and pamphlets about the Black Blocs. Also, the anarchist journal *Rolling Thunder* (*CrimethInc.*) offers stories about Black Bloc actions around the world, written by Black Blockers.

Amster, Randall. *Anarchism Today*. Santa Barbara: Praeger, 2012.

David Van Deusen and Xavier Massot, eds. *The Black Bloc Papers: An Anthology of Primary Texts from the North American Anarchist Black Bloc 1999–2001*. Oakland: AK, 2002.

Day, Richard J.F. *Gramsci Is Dead: Anarchist Currents in the Newest Social Movements*. London: Pluto; Toronto: Between the Lines, 2005.

della Porta, Donatella, and Mario Diani. *Social Movements: An Introduction*. 2nd ed. Oxford: Blackwell, 2006.

Fernandez, Luis A. *Policing Dissent: Social Control and the Anti-Globalization Movement*. New Brunswick: Rutgers University Press, 2008.

Gelderloos, Peter. *How Nonviolence Protects the State*. Cambridge: South End, 2007.

Gordon, Uri. *Anarchy Alive! Anti-Authoritarian Politics from Practice to Theory*. London: Pluto, 2008.

Graeber, David. *Direct Action: An Ethnography*. Oakland: AK, 2009.

Holloway, John, *Change the World Without Taking Power: The Meaning of Revolution Today*. London: Pluto, 2002.

Juris, Jeffrey S. *Networking Futures: The Movements Against Corporate Globalization*. Durham: Duke University Press, 2008.

Kinna, Ruth. *Anarchism*. Oxford: Oneworld, 2005.

Malleson, Tom, and David Wachsmuth, eds. *Whose Streets? The Toronto G20 and the Challenges of Summit Protest*. Toronto: Between the Lines, 2011.

Milstein, Cindy. *Anarchism and Its Aspirations*. Washington: Institute for Anarchist Studies, 2010.

Shantz, Jeff, *Active Anarchy: Political Practice in Contemporary Movements*. Lanham: Lexington, 2011.

Starr, Amory. *Global Revolt: A Guide to the Movements Against Globalization*. London: Zed, 2005.

Starr, Amory, Luis Fernandez, and Christian Scholl, eds. *Shutting Down the Streets: Political Violence and Social Control in the Global Era*. New York: NYU Press, 2011.

Thompson, A.K. *Black Bloc White Riot: Anti-Globalization and the Genealogy of Dissent*. Oakland: AK, 2010.

Waddington, David P. *Policing Public Disorder: Theory and Practice*. London: Routledge, 2012.

Wood, Lesley J. *Direct Action, Deliberation, and Diffusion: Collective Action After the WTO Protests in Seattle*. Cambridge: Cambridge University Press, 2012.

INDEX

About PM Press

politics • culture • art • fiction • music • film

PM Press was founded at the end of 2007 by a small collection of folks with decades of publishing, media, and organizing experience.

We seek to create radical and stimulating media to entertain, educate, and inspire. We aim to distribute these through every available channel with every available technology, whether that means you are seeing anarchist classics at our bookfair stalls; reading our latest vegan cookbook at the café; downloading geeky fiction e-books; or digging new music and timely videos from our website.

Contact us for direct ordering and questions about all PM Press releases, as well as manuscript submissions, review copy requests, foreign rights sales, author interviews, to book an author for an event, and to have PM Press attend your bookfair:

PM Press • PO Box 23912 • Oakland, CA 94623
510-658-3906 • info@pmpress.org • www.pmpress.org

FOPM: MONTHLY SUBSCRIPTION PROGRAM

Friends of PM allows you to directly help impact, amplify, and revitalize the discourse and actions of radical writers and artists. It provides us with a stable foundation to build upon our early successes and provides a much-needed subsidy for the materials that can't necessarily pay their own way. You can help make that happen—and receive every new title automatically delivered to your door once a month. And, we'll throw in a free T-shirt when you sign up.

Here are your options:
- **$30 a month:** Get all books and pamphlets plus 50% discount on all webstore purchases
- **$40 a month:** Get all PM Press releases (including CDs and DVDs) plus 50% discount on all webstore purchases
- **$100 a month:** Superstar—Everything plus PM merchandise, free downloads, and 50% discount on all webstore purchases

For those who can't afford $30 or more a month, we have **Sustainer Rates** at $15, $10 and $5. Sustainers get a free PM Press T-shirt and a 50% discount on all purchases from our website.

Your Visa or Mastercard will be billed once a month, until you tell us to stop. Or until our efforts succeed in bringing the revolution around. Or the financial meltdown of Capital makes plastic redundant. Whichever comes first.